Edward Greey

The bear-worshippers of Yezo and the island of Karafuto

Edward Greey

The bear-worshippers of Yezo and the island of Karafuto

ISBN/EAN: 9783337290924

Printed in Europe, USA, Canada, Australia, Japan

Cover: Foto ©Andreas Hilbeck / pixelio.de

More available books at **www.hansebooks.com**

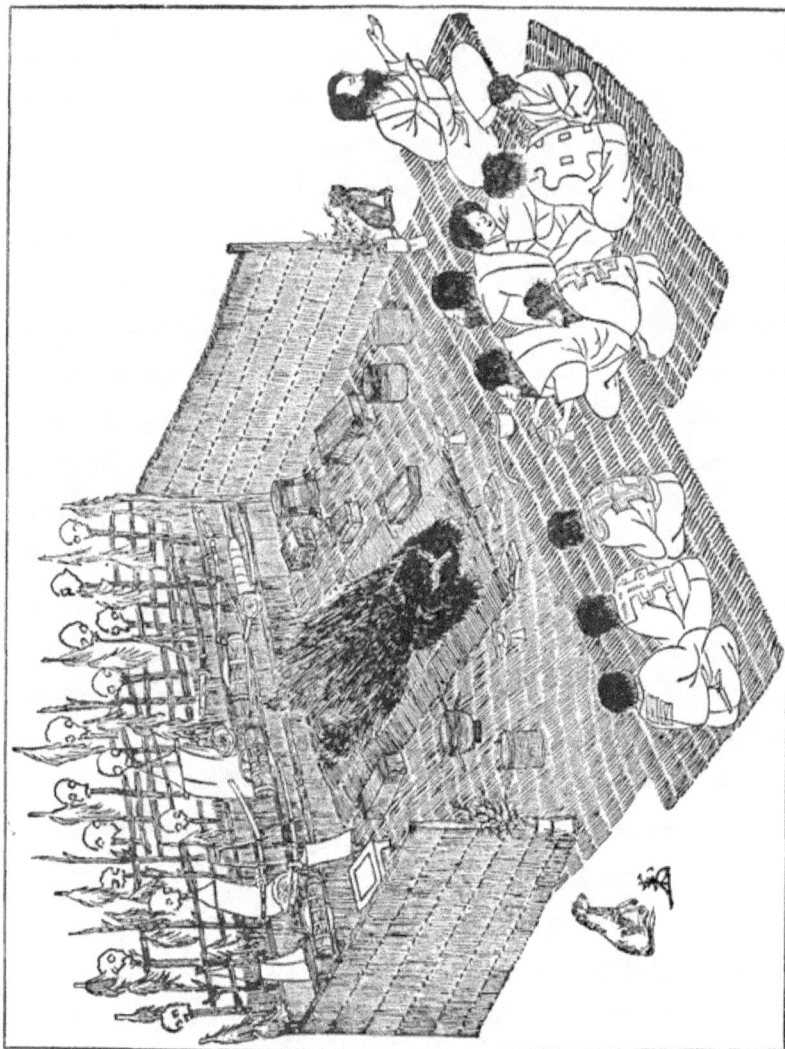

AINOS WORSHIPPING THE BEAR.

THE

BEAR-WORSHIPPERS

OF YEZO

AND THE ISLAND OF KARAFUTO (SAGHALIN)

OR

THE ADVENTURES OF THE JEWETT FAMILY
AND THEIR FRIEND OTO NAMBO

BY

EDWARD GREEY

AUTHOR OF "THE GOLDEN LOTUS." "YOUNG AMERICANS IN JAPAN," "THE WONDERFUL CITY
OF TOKIO," ETC., AND ONE OF THE TRANSLATORS OF THE JAPANESE
ROMANCE "THE LOYAL RONINS"

ONE HUNDRED AND EIGHTY ILLUSTRATIONS BY RINZO AND BY ICHISKE HAMADA

COVER DESIGNED AND DRAWN BY THE AUTHOR

BOSTON
LEE AND SHEPARD, PUBLISHERS
NEW YORK
CHARLES T. DILLINGHAM
1884

PREFACE.

IN "Young Americans in Japan," I gave some account of the southern parts of the empire; and, in "The Wonderful City of Tokio," described the various sights, and the arts and manufactures, for which the capital is famous.

The present volume, the last of the series, is devoted to the manners and customs of the bear-worshippers of Yezo, and of the five tribes inhabiting Karafuto (Saghalin). When I first visited the latter island, in 1853, it was a portion of the Empire of Japan; but in 1875 it was ceded to Russia, in exchange for the Chishima (Kurile) Islands. I spent nearly a year cruising in the northern waters, and during that time became well acquainted with the people of Karafuto and Yezo; on one occasion travelling with a boat's crew from Soya to Hakodate, and being the guest of the fierce-visaged but gentle savages.

Since then Russia has made a penal settlement of Karafuto, and two-thirds of the natives have nominally become Christians.

When I was in Japan, last summer, I made the acquaintance of His Excellency Kunemichi Kitagaki, the governor of Saikio (Kioto), who was for some years an official in the Kaitakushi (Department of Development) of the Hokkaido (North Sea Circuit). From him I learned many interesting particulars relating to the progress made by the Ainos in agriculture, etc.; and I have his authority for stating that the natives who left Karafuto when the island was ceded to Russia, and who have settled in Sapporo, were not compelled to quit their native land, but elected to do so rather than change their nationality.

v

This book was written to give some information concerning a quaint people that are almost unknown to my countrymen, and who, like our Indians, are rapidly disappearing from the face of the earth.

Edward Grsey

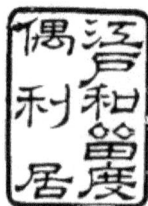

20 EAST 17TH STREET, NEW YORK, 1883.

NOTES.

THE illustrations of this volume are, with a few exceptions, by Japanese artists, and are exceedingly graphic and correct.

I found great difficulty in obtaining pictures of the scenery of such remote places as Yezo and Karafuto, and, but for the assistance and interest taken in the work by many Japanese friends, would have been compelled to relinquish the task. Foremost among those who came to my aid were the Hon. S. K. Takahashi, Japanese consul in this city; and Messrs. K. Okui of the consulate of New York; Tatszgoro Nossé of the Kencho, Yokohama; and Ichiske Hamada of Kagoshima, — to all of whom I return my very best thanks.

Mr. Hamada has also rendered me valuable help in searching various authorities, and in copying some curious pictures, illustrating the peculiar worship of the Ainos, from five *makimono* (scrolls) formerly belonging to a *daimio* of Mito. The woodcuts I have reproduced were taken from three interesting works; viz., "Kita Yezo" (North Yezo), "Higashi Yezo, Yoro monogatari" (Night Stories of Eastern Yezo), and "Karafuto Niki" (Journal of Travel in Karafuto). These volumes also contain much information concerning the inhabitants of the two islands.

To Professor H. S. Munroe, of Columbia College, I am greatly indebted for the loan of a valuable collection of photographs of the Ainos.

The central picture on the cover represents a group of Yezo children engaged in a game played by throwing a hoop into the air, and catching it upon a stick. The bearded savage in the lower corner is an Aino whittling *inaho* (god-sticks). The figure wrestling with a bear is referred to in Chapter VIII. The design in the left upper corner frames the Japanese title *Kuma Matsuri* (literally, Bear-Festival), and upon the red fan I have placed my *kaki-han* (written seal) and my initials.

EDWARD GREEY.

CONTENTS.

ix

ILLUSTRATIONS.

xi

THE

BEAR-WORSHIPPERS.

OF YEZO.

A STREET IN HAKODATE.

THE BEAR-WORSHIPPERS OF YEZO AND SAGHALIN.

CHAPTER I.

BOUND FOR THE FAR NORTH.

" The frog in the well has no idea of the great ocean, still he imagines he knows every thing. Mizuno of Ota had never been out of his native village; yet when he was told about the Yezo-jin (Aino) he laughed, and replied, 'Such tales are very good for children : as for me, I am not acquainted with any one who worships a bear."

THE morning sun was rising over the house-tops at the back of the Jewetts' residence in the Kaga Yashiki, Tokio, as Fitz Jewett summoned his brother and sister, saying, —

"*Hi-yaku*" (hurry up), " Sallie and Johnnie ! Choso's boy, Tatszgoro, is wrestling with little Mankichi ! Do come and take a peep at them."

The young people proceeded to a room overlooking the yard, and, pushing aside the *shoji* (paper-filled window-screen), beheld two Japanese children engaged in what may be termed the national pastime. They had spread a rush mat on the ground, and tied a bamboo across the entrance to the yard in order to keep spectators from approaching too near and interfering with the exhibition.

1

Tatszgoro, whose head was shaven in patches, was a chubby-faced, brown-skinned, black-eyed, merry fellow; and Mankichi was as like him as one bean is to another.

On seeing the Jewetts, Tatszgoro walked round and slapped his limbs like a Japanese wrestler, then crouched on the eastern

TATSZGORO AND MANKICHI WRESTLING.

end of the mat, clinched his fists, and rested upon them and his toes, on all fours.

Mankichi took his place on the western end of the mat, and posed exactly as his comrade had done.

"Shall I be *gioshi?*" (umpire), cried Fitz.

"*Hai, sama!*" (yes, sir), responded the boys, ducking their heads respectfully.

Fitz borrowed his sister's fan, stepped into the veranda, and, addressing the spectators, said, —

" You are about to enjoy a great treat. Tatszgoro is a very skilful wrestler: his fame is known all over our house; he is the champion of the East. Mankichi, who is no less celebrated, is the rampant roarer of the West. Now hold your breath."

" *Hai! hai! hai!*" laughingly responded the lookers-on, among whom were Gosuké and Shobei the *jin-riki-sha* men, old Sokichi the gardener, and the *momban's* wife. The latter wore high clogs, and carried her babe on her back.

While Fitz was speaking, the little wrestlers had remained perfectly still with their eyes respectfully cast downward.

The boy waved his fan, after the manner of the *gioshi*, then said in a commanding voice, —

" *Mi a washi ta tokorode*" (look at each other).

The children obeyed.

" *Sa!*" (begin), he shouted, stepping back a pace.

The contestants rose quickly, grasped one another by the hands, and proceeded to wrestle like the fat athletes at Eko-in.[1]

" Is it not fun!" observed Sallie, who was resting her chin on Johnnie's shoulder. " I do not believe the real *sumotori* do any better."

When Mankichi grasped Tatszgoro incorrectly, Fitz shook his fan, and yelled, —

" *Matai! matai! matai!*" (stop, stop, stop).

On hearing this command, the little fellows relaxed their grip, and retired to their respective places.

After a while Tatszgoro caught Mankichi in a peculiar way, and lifted him off the ground; then suddenly knelt, and pressed his opponent's shoulders flat upon the mat, thus gaining the

[1] *Vide* p. 147, " Wonderful City of Tokio."

victory. This so delighted Fitz, that he danced round and round the combatants, and, taking off his jacket, threw it to Tatszgoro, crying, —

"I will redeem that with ten cents' worth of candy. *Yuké, yuké*" (go on).

Instead of complying, the children rushed in-doors, and the Japanese spectators made off with great precipitation. The young Americans turned to ascertain the cause, and beheld a Yashiki police-man, who was hated by the servants on account of his arrogant ways. He swaggered past the house as though the place belonged to him, and seemed to be suffering from *saké*.

"I do not like that man," said Sallie. "He frightens the children, and the other day he arrested my cat. No wonder the little ones are afraid of him."

THE YASHIKI POLICEMAN.

While they were speaking they heard their father calling for them. Presently Professor Jewett and his wife entered the room; and the former said, —

"I have news for you. A government steamer leaves for Yezo at four o'clock, and we are going in her. Make haste: there is no time to lose."

"I have had my trunk packed for the last month, sir," said Fitz. "We are ready to go right away."

At noon the Professor and his family started in their *jin-*

riki-sha for the Shimbashi depot, a dozen servants following
with the baggage.

They took the train for Yokohama, and arrived at the settlement about two o'clock. The Professor, being upon government duty, was met by Capt. Imadate, who escorted them to
his boat, which was lying alongside the English *hatoba* (wharf).

Soon they were being rowed swiftly to the Japanese man-of-
war, in which they were to embark,
and within an hour were steaming
down the Bay of Yedo.

The vessel was entirely officered
and manned by Nihonese, and the
discipline was perfect. There was a
detachment of troops on board ; and
as soon as the vessel was under way,
the soldiers were mustered, and the
roll called.

" How badly their clothes fit
them ! " remarked Fitz. " The pants
look as though they were made by
machinery."

" They can fight, spite of their
clumsy looks," retorted Johnnie.

JAPANESE INFANTRY SOLDIER.

" After all, I have seen foreign soldiers who were not any better
dressed than these, and who could not fight a bit."

The men were drilled, then dismissed ; after which the
colonel approached the Jewetts, and said, —

" We are going to land at Sendai, and shall not have the
pleasure of accompanying you to Hakodate. Do you know
that your friend Dr. Nambo will join you there ? He embarked
by the steamer that preceded us."

"Yes, I am aware that the doctor will be one of our party," answered the Professor. "I do not believe my family would enjoy the trip north unless our friend accompanied us."

"For what are we slowing up?" inquired Fitz; "and why are the people clustering in the bow?"

"Come and see," said the colonel. "I think we have stopped in order to avoid running down a fishing-craft."

They went forward, and beheld a most interesting sight, — fishermen hauling in their net, which was alive with enormous *karei* (flounders) and crabs. The men worked with a will, and soon the gigantic net was drawn on board; then sail was trimmed, and the *fune* (junk) and steamer rapidly parted company.

THE KIRIN.

"We should starve without those fellows," said the captain. "There is not a mile of water belonging to the Japanese Empire that is not searched for food. We pride ourselves upon the ability of our fishermen."

"Dinner is ready, *Sama*," said the captain's steward, saluting respectfully.

"And so am I!" exclaimed Fitz. "The salt air has made me very hungry."

Upon descending to the saloon they found the table spread in foreign fashion, and soon every one was enjoying the repast.

"Why do you have the *kirin* carved upon the woodwork?" inquired Johnnie.

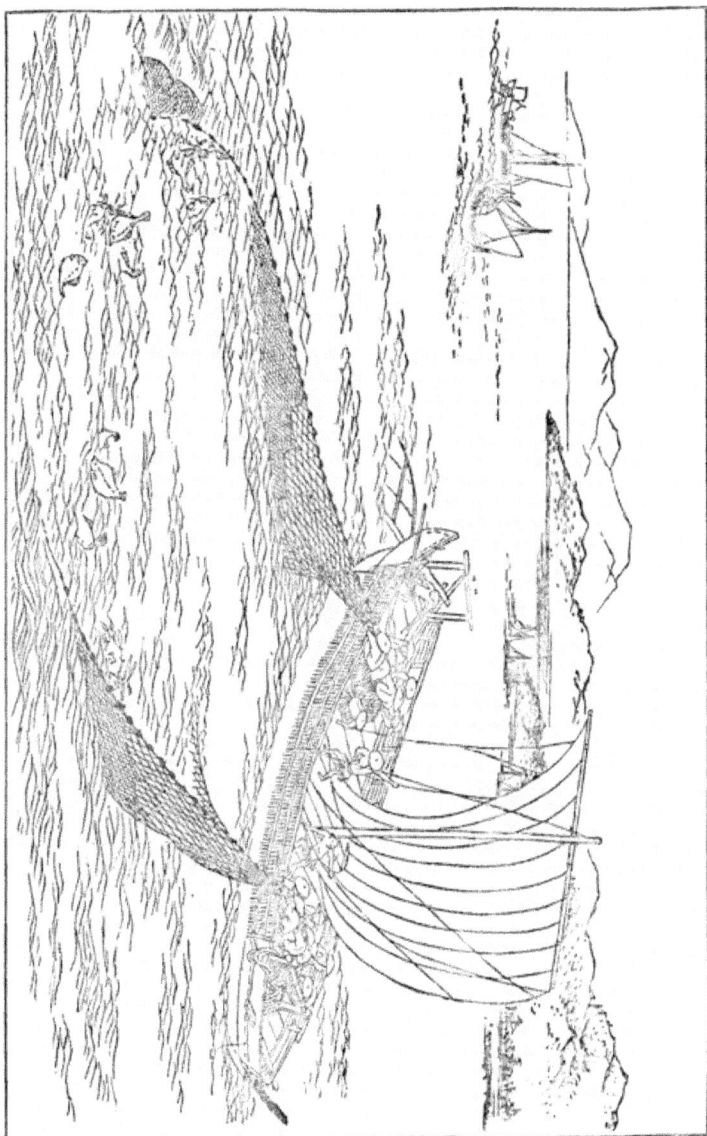

FISHING FOR TURBOT.

"It is often used in conjunction with the *kiri-mon*" (imperial crest), answered the commander. "Some people believe it to be the guardian of the imperial family. Being a sailor, I do not know much about these things."

After dinner they adjourned to the quarter-deck, and listened to the band, which entertained them with native and foreign airs.

At ten o'clock they retired; and soon the thud of the screw, and the lapping of the waves against the ship's side, were the only sounds that broke the stillness of the night.

About two A.M., Fitz awoke, and, looking through the port, saw lights flickering upon the water; whereupon he roused his brother, remarking, —

"Say, Johnnie, let us go on deck and see the fun. We are approaching a narrow channel between the mainland and some islands, and I want to learn how those fellows work their torches."

The lads put on their Japanese *kimono*, which they wore as dressing-gowns, and proceeded up the companion-ladder; at the top of which they were greeted by the first lieutenant, who said, —

"*Ohayo !*" ("you are early," equivalent to our "good-morning.") "Are your beds too hard?"

"Oh, no!" answered Johnnie. "This scene is too interesting to miss."

They approached the ship's side, and, as the vessel threaded her way among the boats, watched the fishermen at their occupation.

In the bow of each craft was an iron cresset, that projected about a yard from the side, and in which burned pine-knots and other inflammable kindling, that flared and attracted the

FISHING, BY TORCHLIGHT.

fishes. The men all wore broad bamboo hats and blue cotton shirts, and had straw coats tied about their waists. They fished with lines, and the sinkers were tied within a foot of the hooks. When a big fish was caught, the captor would yell exultingly, and boast about the size of his prize.

"Phew!" said Fitz, "what an unpleasant odor!"

"It is the clams they use for bait," said the first lieutenant. "The fish like them when they are very stale."

"So I should think," grimly observed Johnnie.

The air was too cool to allow them to remain on deck with any pleasure : so the boys presently returned to their beds, and

JAPANESE CAVALRY SOLDIER.

were soon once more fast asleep.

When they awoke they found that the vessel was running along the coast, which was very romantic and beautiful.

On the morning of the second day they anchored in the Bay of Sendai, and the American party went on shore.

Upon approaching the landing-place, they were saluted by Dr. Oto Nambo, who said, imitating the New-England drawl of an old fisherman at Cromlech, —

"We——ll, I thought you was never coming."

"Who is your friend?" asked Johnnie in English, indicating a soldier who was seated on the wharf behind Oto.

"He is a cavalryman, one of my patients," said Oto jocosely. "Do not be rude to me, or he may cut off your head. He was formerly a *ronin*."

"I should think so," said Fitz. "In the olden times the

ronin disguised themselves by wearing hats that concealed
their faces : now they are completely lost in their boots."

"Do hush, Fitz," whispered Sallie. "Perhaps he can understand English."

Oto helped them on shore, then said, —

"I am real glad to see you all. The ship will remain here
for a day, so you will have time to visit the *awabi* fishery."

A STREET IN SENDAI.

"What a queer old street!" said Sallie, as they ascended the
main thoroughfare. "I should die if I had to live in such a
place as this."

"Then you would not have to live here," quietly answered
Johnnie. "Sallie is always going to die when every thing is
not in apple-pie order."

They ascended the steps of the street, and, turning to the
left, entered a Japanese *yadoya* (inn), where they found an
excellent repast had been prepared for them.

"Oh, baked beans!" shouted the irrepressible. "This is what I call a civilized place."

When the meal was over, the party engaged *jin-riki-sha*, and rode along the coast until they reached the scene of the *awabi* fishery, — a rocky promontory round which were moored a number of boats.

Professor Jewett, who was somewhat fond of lecturing, turned to his children, and said, —

"The *awabi*, or rather the *haliotis tuberculata*, commonly called the sea-ear, is a univalve shell-fish, which is gathered from the sides of rocks that are always submerged."

"Please spare us, Professor," murmured Mrs. Jewett, who feared a prolonged dissertation on conchology. "I believe the children are pretty well posted."

"Yes, mother," said Fitz, with a nod. "We have had all the varieties of *haliotis* for breakfast, tiffin, and dinner. Guess we will recognize them when we see them."

The Professor stroked his beard, but did not continue his remarks; then, seating himself upon the rocks, watched the fishing.

The boats were secured close to the shore, and were already somewhat heavily laden with *awabi*. Each craft carried two divers; excepting the one at the extreme end of the point, from which Oto informed them a man had been lost on the previous day. "Eaten by an *octopus*" (devil-fish), he sententiously remarked. "That is his little boy in the boat : do you not notice how sad he looks?"

The divers wore what Fitz termed straw waistcoats : otherwise they were lightly clad. They stood in the bows of their boats, and, after securing ropes about their bodies, dived headlong into the waves. Each carried an iron instrument in his girdle with which to detach the *awabi* from the rocks.

FISHING FOR AWABI.

The Americans watched the men with great interest, and saw them crawl along the bottom of the sea and secure the coveted prizes.   Upon reaching the surface they handed the fish to their comrades, who put them in baskets, and commented as follows : —

"That is a very large one," or otherwise : " I like a man who keeps his eyes open under water.   Now, good friend, take a long breath, and descend again.   The days are short, and we want to make all the money we can."

The party spent about an hour seeing the divers, then followed Oto to a nook in which men, women, and children were busy preparing the *awabi* for market.

When the boats filled with fish were landed on the beach, they were unloaded by men, who, as they worked, uttered loud cries, and bore the baskets to mats spread upon the sand.

The *awabi* has gristly flesh, like a little-neck clam.   The fish that are not despatched fresh to the market are pared, like apples, into long strips, which are laid on mats, and dried in the sun and air.

Everybody was very busy, — some paring, others spreading the strips on mats, and the remainder of the party packing the dried fish.   All were full of fun, and seemed to make a picnic of the business.

The scene was certainly an animated one ; but the odor was not pleasant, so the spectators did not remain very long.

As they walked back to Sendai, Sallie remarked, —

" I do not believe your fishermen possess the sense of smell, or they never could bear what they do."

" Oh ! I do not know so much about that," quietly responded Oto.   " I recollect feeling quite overpowered by the perfume of the menhaden-oil factories of Gloucester."

PREPARING AWABI FOR THE MARKET.

"Yes," said Fitz, with a chuckle. "Do you remember, when you remarked about the scent, the proprietor told you that the money he earned by the business was sweet?"

Sallie smiled, nodded, and said, —

"I suppose there is really not much difference between the Japanese and American fish-business."

Upon turning a point of the coast, they beheld a most animated scene. Four boats, manned by lightly clad fishermen, were working a net in which they had just made a haul of *tai*, a kind of shad. The net was secured to two boats, and the fish were being taken from it with scoops shaped like those used to catch butterflies. As one boat was filled, it was rowed to the shore, emptied, and hurried back to the scene of operation.

"Gracious! are they not excited?" exclaimed Sallie.

"There is money in it," said Johnnie, "Each *tai* is worth five *sen* to the men. They do not make such a haul every day. You shout, do you not, when you catch a fish?"

"No, she screams," said Fitz. "She says, 'I cannot touch it! Take it away: it will bite me!'"

"Do not tease me, brother," pleaded Sallie. "You know I dislike to give any thing pain."

"Come," said the Professor, "I think we had better be moving. I do not know how you feel: I am hungry."

"Well, sir, I would not object to a planked shad myself," said Fitz. "I vote we secure some."

Upon asking the fishermen the price, they said one *yen* (dollar) each, and they would not take any less.

"Then we will go without," said Mrs. Jewett. "I think it is an imposition to ask more here than they do in the Tokio market."

As the party moved away, the fishermen called out, —

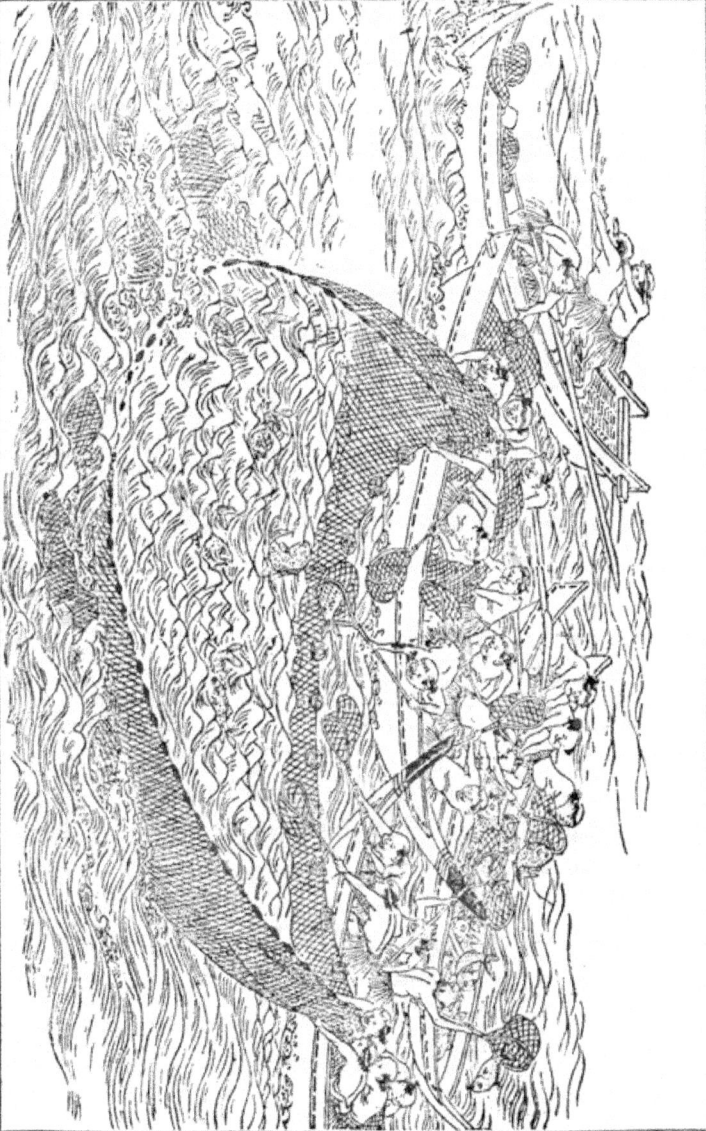

" You may have as many as you want for ten cents each."

When the foreigners had gone a little distance, a woman ran after them with a string of the finest *tai*, and, smiling, said, —

" Please accept these, and give us any thing you like."

" Give her a *chit*" (note to be paid by their house-steward in Tokio), said Fitz.

Every one laughed at this; and a bargain was made with the woman, who, for twenty-five *sen*, agreed to carry the *tai* to Sendai.

When the travellers neared the town, they noticed a great many rows of stakes driven in the water along the flat portions of the shore.

" Those are oyster and mussel farms," said Oto. " Millions of bushels are annually raised in this manner. Tall bamboos are driven into the mud, and formed into barriers, to which the shell-fish readily attach themselves. When the tide is coming in, the doors of the enclosures are opened; and as soon as it begins to turn, they are closed again in order to cut off the retreat of the fishes. At low water the owners of the pound enter it, and secure their victims, and rake off whatever shell-fish they require. This method is pursued all round the coast of Japan and Yezo, and is a source of great wealth; the oyster-farmers paying a tax to the government."

" It seems to me, in Japan, every thing pays a tax to the government," remarked Fitz.

" Yes, we tax a good many articles," quietly replied Oto; " and so do you, if my memory serves me rightly. I think it ought to convince you how closely we have copied American customs."

Fitz whistled, then made a grimace as though he wished he had not spoken.

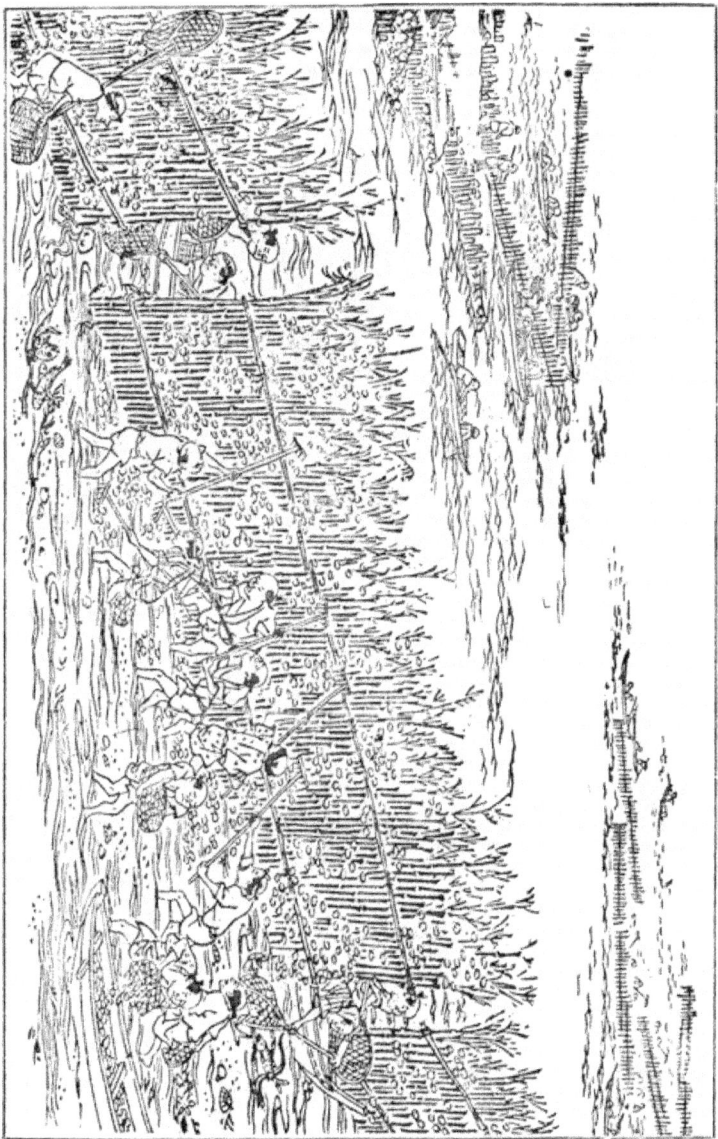

SHELL-FISH CULLING.

They soon after entered their *jin-riki-sha*, and were rapidly conveyed to the inn; on nearing which the Professor sniffed, and remarked, —

"I smell the odor of the *serranus marginalis*."

His surmise proved to be correct; among the dishes served being a fine specimen of the *tai* they had seen caught that afternoon.

At ten o'clock the next morning the party re-embarked on board the man-of-war, and started up the coast.

CHAPTER II.

HAKODATE.

"Fresh air is a very excellent thing. One enjoys plenty of this in the chief city of Yezo, where, in order to keep a roof over their heads, the people have to cover the shingles with huge rocks.

"It is said, when Futen (the god of the winds) unties his bag, he always points its neck in the direction of Hakodate."

THE Americans landed at several places along the coast, so the ship did not reach Tsugaru Strait until the afternoon of the third day.

As they neared Yezo, they saw a cluster of islands, on one of which were two *torii* and a little temple.

"That, to the left, is Benten-shima," said Oto. "The one behind it is Obi-shima. The sailors go to Benten's temple to say their last prayer before they proceed to sea, the queen of the ocean being their patroness."

"Why do those *fune* (junks) have diamond-shaped marks on their sails?"

"That was one of the badges of the Lord of Matsumai," replied the young doctor. "Although the title of *daimio* is abolished, these old-fashioned captains of junks still carry the crest of their former chief on their sails. They are mostly ignorant men who do not read the newspapers."

"In which direction is Hakodate?" inquired Sallie.

"Round the point to the right," answered Oto. "We shall probably come to anchor in about an hour."

They chatted with the officers, who told them that the vessel expected to take the party to Karafuto (Saghalin), the most northerly of the two islands, and that the captain had received orders to convey the Professor to whatever part of Yezo he decided to visit.

"Look at those big fish!" excitedly exclaimed Sallie, pointing to a school of whales making into the harbor.

"We call them Aino beef," said Oto. "The savages on the coast would die if it were not for those creatures; besides,

BENTEN-SHIMA AND OBI-SHIMA.

there is a great business done in exporting the dried flesh to Japan, and in the oil which is sold to foreigners."

"You speak as though you were no longer in your native country," said Mrs. Jewett.

Oto changed color, and replied, —

"Indeed, this is not Japan. It is merely a dependency which we colonize and protect."

"You mean rule," said the matter-of-fact Fitz. "England has seized India under the plea of protecting it."

"Yezo is not like India," said the Professor: "it is really a

portion of great Japan, peopled by an aboriginal race ; " adding
with a sly glance at Oto, " I do not mean to assert that your
ancestors were Ainos."

As they neared Hakodate, they saw that the city consisted
of long, straggling streets at the base of a tolerably high hill ;
the harbor being formed by a neck of land, something like
Marblehead on the eastern shore of Massachusetts.

Numbers of *fune* (junks) were moored off the point ; some
American whalers, British men-of-war, and foreign merchant-
ships were anchored in the harbor ; and the water was alive
with native boats propelled by scantily costumed *sendo* (boatmen), who, as they passed the vessel, shouted a welcome to
the new-comers.

The Jewetts disembarked in a ship's-boat, and were taken
to the residence of one of Oto's relatives, who welcomed them,
and placed his house at their disposition.

" Where are the Ainos?" inquired Sallie. " I expected to
see lots of them on the streets."

Mr. Yamamoto, their host, who had spent some years in
the States, smiled as though very much amused ; then, bowing,
said, —

" We have very few Ainos in Hakodate, and just at present those are away fishing. We treat them as you do your
Indians."

" Kill them off, eh ? " said Fitz.

" Oh, no ! " gently answered Mr. Yamamoto. " What I
meant was this : We are gradually colonizing this island, and
endeavoring to reclaim it for agricultural purposes : however, in
doing so, we have no desire to exterminate the Ainos, who are
very harmless people."

" That is most humane of you," said Mrs. Jewett. " I think

it is much better to try and improve the condition of savages, than to goad them into desperation, and shoot them down when they rebel."

"Dinner is served, *Sama*," said Mr. Yamamoto's chief servant, who during the conversation had entered the doorway, where he knelt and bowed his head to the mats.

"Please follow me," said their host, leading the way to an adjoining apartment. "I regret to have to offer you such poor entertainment, but up here in Yezo one has to suffer many hardships."

As he ended his speech he bowed, drew in his breath politely, and conducted them into a room where they found a table spread in American fashion.

The Jewetts thoroughly enjoyed their repast; at the conclusion of which Mr. Yamamoto asked them to visit his library, which was filled with the best foreign and Japanese works.

Fitz halted before a picture on the wall, and inquired, —

"Will you please tell me what this represents?"

"Yes, with pleasure," answered their new friend. "Many years ago three *ronin samurai* arrived in Aomori on their way to this city. They were pursued by some of the Shogun's soldiers, who had orders to bring back their heads. The people of Aomori did not favor the *ronin*, and the fishermen refused to take them across the strait. In their desperation they proceeded as far as Omasaki. Presently they saw behind them in the distance the soldiers of the Shogun, who had tracked them from Yedo. This sight made the poor fellows desperate, and they concluded to die rather than surrender. As they rushed down to the water's edge, they beheld an Aino boat rising and falling on the billows.

"'Let us swim out to it,' said the leader. 'We will seize the craft which the gods have sent us.'

HAKODATE FROM THE SEA.

"In another moment they were making their way through the surf; while their pursuers stood on the strand, and vainly discharged arrows at the fugitives. Upon nearing the boat, an Aino rose in the stern, and, regarding them with amazement, inquired, —

"'What do you want?'

"As neither of the *ronin* understood the Aino tongue, they scrambled on board, and pointed toward Yezo.

"The chief nodded his head, seized his paddle, walked forward, and began to prod at what looked like six brown sacks lying in the bow. These proved to be as many Aino women, who, rousing from their slumber, grasped the line attached to the stone that served for an anchor, and dragged the heavy weight from the bottom.

"After much exertion they were ready to start, and, taking up their paddles, headed the craft for Hakodate.

"This picture was painted by a friend of mine named Jiu-bu."

"I do not think he was a very great artist," critically observed Fitz. "It appears all of a jobble."

"It represents a jobbling sea," said Sallie.

"What is jobble?" inquired their host.

"It means water twisting and tumbling as that does. You won't find the word in the dictionary: it was invented by a tea-merchant in Yokohama."

"Ah!" sighed Mr. Yamamoto, "the tea-merchants of Yokohama have added some extraordinary words to the language of *Dai Nihon*."

The evening was passed in looking over pictures, and chatting about their prospective trip into the interior.

Professor Jewett consulted with the captain of the man-of-

AINO RESCUING RONIN.

war, and finally decided to wait a day or two in Hakodate, then proceed to Nikamori, whence they would penetrate northward, and re-embark at Diakotan for Saghalin.

The next morning they went out to see the sights of Hakodate, a city said to contain thirty-seven thousand people.

" I do not know where they all are," remarked Johnnie. " I think they must be stowed away indoors. This is a deadly lively place."

JAPANESE POLICEMAN AND AINO.

" Hullo ! " exclaimed Fitz, as they neared a ward division. " What is that policeman looking at? He appears to be mightily puzzled."

His friends glanced at the official, who was regarding a man crouching in the street, with the greatest curiosity ; the police-man having only that day arrived in the island.

"That is a Yezo-jin" (Aino), answered Mr. Yamamoto. " He is as much amazed as the new-comer. The officer will soon get used to such sights, and will make the Aino obey him. Would you like to visit the post-office and custom-house?"

"I would rather go to the theatre," said Fitz. "Is not that one ahead, on our left?" pointing to a low building, the eaves of which were adorned with highly colored pictures, representing scenes in plays, which a man was repairing, and tying to the frame-work.

"There is no performance this week," said Mr. Yamamoto. "Our only amusements, just now, are some celebrated fencers from Tokio, who exhibit this afternoon."

The shops were filled with miscellaneous articles; among which were beautiful bear and dog skins, and some clumsy imitations of American canned provisions.

None of the houses were high. All were of wood; and the shingles of the roofs were held down by enormous stones, an inexpensive way of securing them during the gales for which the region is famous.

Notwithstanding Fitz's objection, they visited the hospital, which was under the charge of Dr. Fucasi, a very able surgeon, who was assisted by six graduates of the Imperial College of Tokio.

"We have accommodation for over a hundred patients," said the doctor; "and we use foreign beds. All the arrangements were planned by a well-known American physician and surgeon, — Dr. Stuart Eldridge of Yokohama. We are greatly indebted to him for many things."

He conducted them through the buildings; and, on arriving at the reception-room for patients, said, —

"I have two Ainos waiting to consult me. Would you like to see them?"

"Yes," answered the Professor. "My boys are most anxious to interview the Yezo-jin."

Dr. Fucasi ushered them into the apartment, where they

beheld two stout-looking savages, clothed in garments made of
brown fibre obtained from the bark of a tree; portions of the
dresses being decorated with blue bands embroidered with
white cotton. Their faces were not like the Japanese: their
hair was very soft, and somewhat wavy; their eyebrows, mustaches, and beards were
thick and heavy; their foreheads high, broad, and mas-
sive ; their frames strong
and well knit; their noses
flat, and their mouths wide ;
and, though their unkempt
hair gave them a somewhat
ferocious look, their manners were gentle, and their
voices singularly low and
musical.

On seeing the visitors,
they saluted them by ex-
tending their hands and
waving them towards their
faces.

The elder of the Ainos,
who was a chief, carried a
bow and arrows; to the quiver of which were fastened a number
of *inaho* (god-sticks), without which these strange people never
think of travelling.

The *inaho* is made of a piece of pine-wood whittled in a
peculiar way, so as to leave it covered with tiny curled shavings. It is their idea of a god, and their charm to ward off
danger. No Aino knows its origin, or do any two of them

AINOS.

[FROM PHOTOGRAPH LOANED BY PROF. MUNROE.]

use it in exactly the same manner. It is possibly a relic of an ancient religion, and is not in any way related to the *gohei* of Japan.

The men, being the first natives seen closely by the Americans, were objects of great interest to the young people, who put a number of questions to them; Dr. Fucasi acting as interpreter.

The chief said they had no written characters for their language, and consequently possessed no books; that they believed in good and bad *kami* (gods), and that in order to please them they ought to drink plenty of *saké* (rice-wine).

"That is a very Western belief," said Mrs. Jewett. "Many of our people are more devoted to the evil spirit of wine than to the spirit of truth."

"It shows that the Ainos are civilized," said the Professor. "I am afraid intemperance is a disease common to poor humanity of all nations."

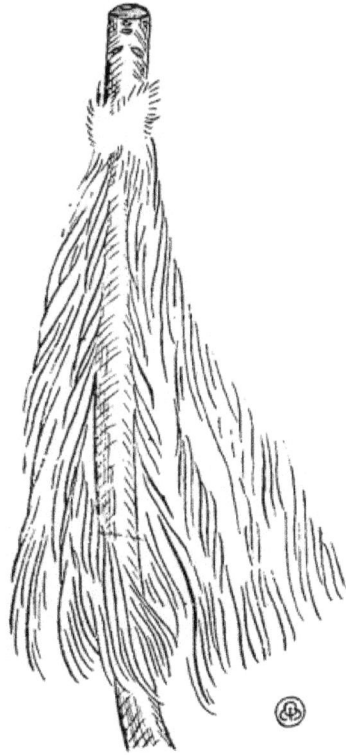

INAHO.

Dr. Fucasi conducted the party to his residence, where he entertained them with tea and cakes.

"What was the origin of the Aino?" inquired Johnnie.

The doctor smiled, then said, —

"Once upon a time, when the gods lived on the earth,

a beautiful goddess appeared off Yezo in a boat. She was
accompanied by a faithful dog, who had been with her in all
her wanderings."

" Did he steer the craft?" inquired Fitz.

" The fact is not recorded," answered the doctor, whose
eyes twinkled with fun. " They probably performed the duty
by turns."

" Please don't interrupt, brother," said Sallie. " The legend
is very interesting."

Dr. Fucasi continued, —

" Upon landing, the lady sought shelter in a cave, where she
spent her time in writing poems and in weeping. There,"
pointing to a *kakémono* on the wall, " is a representation of the
scene. You will notice the faithful dog is bringing her a fish."

" It must have been rather an uncomfortable place for her
to camp in," said Fitz. " I would have launched the boat
again, and gone to a place where there were houses. She
appears to have let down her back hair, and to have abandoned
herself to grief."

" No doubt the true interpretation of the legend is this,"
said the doctor. " One of the princesses of Japan was, with
her attendants, banished to this island, where she was well
received by the natives, who called themselves Aino. This
sounds like our Japanese word *inu* (dog), hence the story that
a faithful dog fed the unhappy goddess. I believe we Japanese invented the tale, and first told the Yezo-jin of their curious
origin. The natives say, 'The Aino man is as strong, fierce, and
brave as a dog; and that the Aino woman is as gentle as the
kami from whom she is descended.'"

" I presume it is a sort of Darwinism," said the Professor.
" Doctor, what are the principal characteristics of the Aino?"

GODDESS AND HER FAITHFUL ATTENDANT.

"They are, when sober, good-tempered and kindly; but, as a rule, lazy, and inclined to take life easily. I never knew one of them to suffer from a nervous disorder."

They took leave of the doctor, and returned to their friend's house, where they met some of the officials of the *Kaitakushi*, i.e., the department for the improvement of Yezo, which island is termed by the Japanese Government the *Hokkaido*, or North Sea Circuit.

One of them had brought a *sho-mon* (passport) from the governor, which gave the Professor and his party special privileges, and instructed all officials to entertain and assist him.

When the visitors had retired, Oto said to the boys, —

"Let us go and see the fencing. It is good fun, and I am sure your mother and sister will excuse us."

"I will accompany you," said the Professor. "These exhibitions always interest me."

They walked down the street, and soon arrived at a house above which was a sign inscribed, —

"Great artists from Tokio. Wonderful exhibition of fencing with swords, spears, and other weapons. By permission of his excellency the governor. Admission five *rin*" (half a cent).

"This is a very inexpensive entertainment," said Professor Jewett, as he tendered his money.

"Would your excellency like private seats for your party?" asked the ticket-seller. "The price for such accommodation is only one *yen*" (dollar).

The offer was accepted; and they entered the building, a barn-like shell, in the centre of which was a raised structure, loosely floored with planks.

Near the stage stood a young man, partly dressed in armor, whose head bristled like a field of young rice, who wore American spectacles and a *samurai* sword, and who was producing most doleful noises from an enormous conch-shell.

Fitz regarded him ruefully, then said to Oto, —

"He toots that horn more persistently than old Jem, who sells clams at Cromlech; does he not?"

"Yes," answered the young doctor. "It is hard work. Here come the fencers."

Two lads and an old man mounted the stage, and, kneeling in a row, bowed respectfully, until their foreheads touched the boards. Then the elder, half rising, leaned upon his fan, and said in a sing-song voice, —

"Tanaka and Nakayama. Two of the most celebrated fencers in Tokio. They will now give an exhibition with

PERFORMER ON THE CONCH SHELL.

the *shine*" (bamboo-staff) "and the *kama*" (bamboo-sickle). The combatants then rose, and proceeded to array themselves for the fray.

First they put on *hakama* (trousers), then breastplates and waist-armor, after which they donned thickly wadded helmets and masks and gloves.

The master of the ceremonies, who was comically precise

in his actions, regarded them paternally, and, when they were
accoutred, signalled them to attack. They danced round, and
struck one another in a very lively fashion, but did not appear
to mind taking punishment.

Fitz, as usual, became excited, and at the conclusion of a

JAPANESE FENCING.

rally, when the bamboos had given out sparks, threw his hat on
to the platform, shouting, —

"That is good for a dollar;" meaning he would redeem it
at the price named after the exhibition was over.

The Professor frowned, and observed, "My son, do not be
so impulsive. Such an act is not dignified."

The boy's face flushed; and he murmured, "Thought, after
whacking each other like that, the poor fellows ought to have
some little encouragement."

The entertainment terminated with a passage-at-arms between the master of the ceremonies and four of his pupils, which afforded the greatest amusement to the young Americans.

As the party quitted the building, they noticed a bird perched on the neighboring fence, making a great chatter.

" That is a *karasu*" (crow), said Oto. " They are great thieves, and are quite common in this island."

" We have them at home," said Johnnie. " I kept a tame one for a long time. He stole Sallie's earrings, and gave us a good deal of trouble. Do your crows do such things?"

" No," gravely answered Oto : " they are not civilized enough for that ;" adding, " They con-
fine their attention to hunting for food, and have no taste for jewelry."

They returned to their friend's house, and spent the evening in superintending the packing of provisions, etc., for the journey through the interior.

YEZO CROW.

" You will be able to se-
cure the services of any number of Ainos," remarked Mr. Yamamoto : " they are very docile, and can carry great burdens."

On the following day the party inspected the prison, and were very much interested in all they saw.

The inmates work at various trades, do engraving and paint-
ing, and manufacture perfumery, candles, soap, and furniture. They appeared to be very comfortable, received pay for all their labor, and were charged for the cost of their maintenance ; the balance of their earnings being handed to them when their sen-
tences expire. The prison uniform was a red *kimono*, which

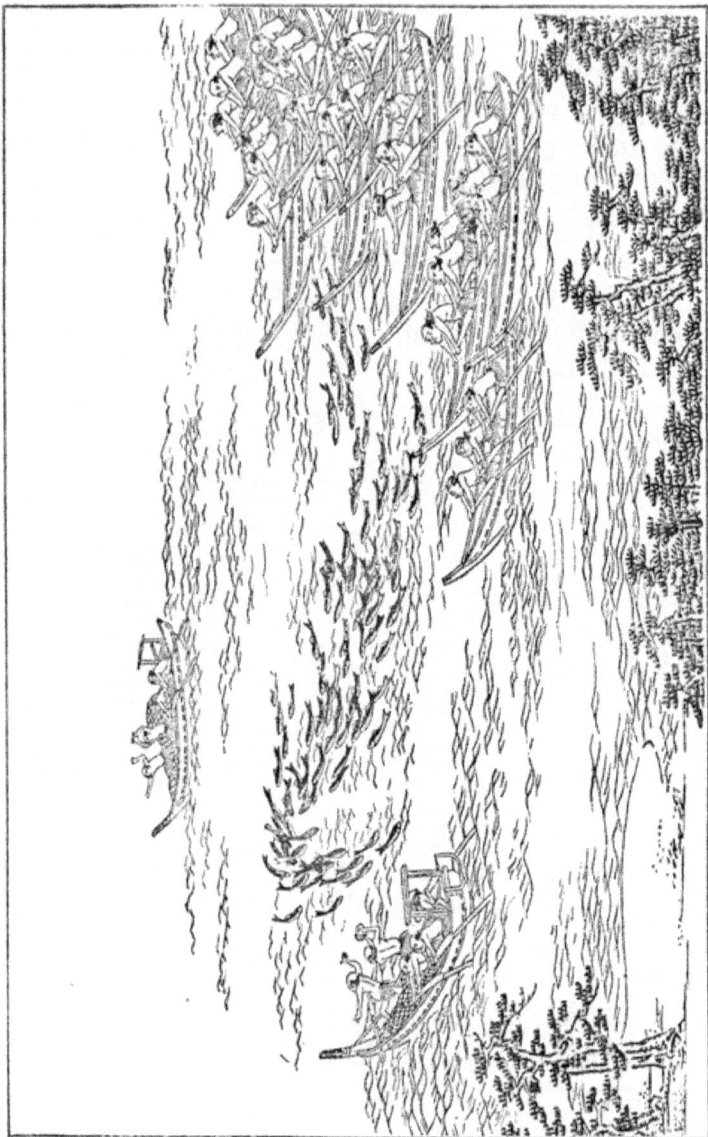

DRIVING SAWARA.

color was therefore not popular among their fellow-townsmen. Certainly no nation can accuse the Japanese of treating their prisoners harshly.

After visiting the principal temple, the Americans returned to Mr. Yamamoto's house, and devoted their time to writing home.

" The Mitsu-bishi steamer leaves to-morrow for Yokohama," said the Professor, addressing his children. " It will be your last chance for many a long day. We shall probably spend two months in the interior : so write to the good folks at Cromlech, and tell them they need not expect to hear from you before June or July."

Upon the following morning, the party re-embarked in the man-of-war, and steamed across Volcano Bay.

" We shall touch at one or two places before we land you," said the captain. " I have to visit several fishing-stations."

Towards noon they came in sight of a number of boats, driving *sawara*, a sort of Spanish mackerel. The fishermen rowed with their faces to the bow, and yelled vociferously, hurling great stones, and splashing the water in order to head the fish in the required direction. When this was accomplished, they joined two nets together, and, surrounding the school, contrived to capture the whole of it.

The vessel touched at Yubets, where there was quite a large fishing-station, and where the travellers had an opportunity of seeing the working of the big seines used in capturing *buri*. The net must have been half a mile long ; and it was dragged towards the shore by stout cables attached to upright windlasses worked by Japanese, no Ainos being employed by the company who owned that part of the coast.

As the ends of the seine neared the beach, fishermen

FISHING FOR BURI.

stationed in boats inside the lines rattled bamboos fastened to the top of poles, shouted, and clapped pieces of wood together, in order to drive the *buri* into the body of the net. It was a most animated scene, — the fish jumping in schools from the water, their stomachs flashing in the sun ; the boatmen ply-ing their instruments, and uttering savage cries ; and the men at the capstan straining and tugging as though their future happiness depended upon their exertions.

The voyagers proceeded from Yubets to Mombets ; passing on the way a fleet of boats engaged in catching a large species of blackfish, which were dried and sent to Kobe and Tokio.

One of the craft boarded the man-of-war ; and the fisher-men presented the captain with several *buri*, that flapped about on the deck as though desirous of returning to their native element.

Mombets proved to be a mean-looking place, occupied by Japanese and Aino fishermen in about equal numbers.

The American party landed, and saw the process of drying *buri*, and making oil of a species of menhaden, which were tried out in a pan set over a charcoal-fire. The oil spattered in all directions, and the fish were put in the pan by suspending them from the end of a long bamboo set in a revolving post. Drift-wood was used as fuel ; but, being saturated with salt water, it did not burn very freely.

A long-tailed rooster was perched on the top of one of the houses, sunning and drying his plumage.

Mombets, like all similar villages, was mal-odorous, and did not offer any inducements for the party to linger there.

They continued along the coast, which was lined with fish-ing-stations that gave abundant evidence of the perseverance, enterprise, and intelligence of the Japanese.

SEINING BLACKFISH.

MOMBETS.

The ship ran close enough to the shore to enable the travellers to witness many very interesting sights.

At one place an enormous seine filled with *katsu* was being hauled up the beach, and its flapping contents thrown into frames placed over furnaces fitted with pans of water which were steaming at a great rate. When the *katsu* were thoroughly cooked, they were boned, and the flesh dried upon mats spread upon the sand.

The floats on the nets used in capturing *katsu* were made in the shape of little barrels, and were buoyant enough to prevent the seines from being drawn under water by the powerful fish.

"There is an Aino hunting!" cried Johnnie, pointing to a shock-headed, bearded figure upon a rocky promontory. "Look! he has just discharged an arrow, and is watching to see if he has secured a prize."

The savage noticed them, then hid himself among the bamboo grass, like a bashful child, and did not re-appear as long as the vessel was in sight.

"You will see enough of them before you come on board again," said the captain. "For my part, I think they are little better than animals. That fellow could drink as much *saké* as any ten Japanese."

"Are you a teetotaller, captain?" innocently inquired Sallie.

This made the commander smile; and he answered,—

"Oh, no! I only recommend it for the Ainos. *Saké* does them a great deal of harm: for myself, I take it medicinally."

"We are in sight of Nikamori," reported the first lieutenant.

"Will you land this evening?" inquired the commander of the Professor. "I fear you will find the accommodation very

STEAMING KATSU.

poor. My advice is, that you stay with me, and disembark early to-morrow morning."

"Very many thanks," said the Professor. " I will follow your suggestion."

When the anchor was let go, the party went forward, and gazed at the shore.

NIKAMORI.

"So that is Nikamori," said Fitz. "Well, it is a rough-looking spot, and I do not see any Ainos."

"Wait a while," said Oto. " Before the week is over we shall be pretty well acquainted with the bear-worshippers."

AINO HUNTING. (*Vide* p. 41.)

CHAPTER III.

AMONG THE AINOS.

"Every one has a certain amount of native conceit, that is oftentimes ridiculous in the eyes of strangers. The Yezo-jin say, 'The Ainos will always be the pride of the sea and the forest.'"

AT daybreak the boys were aroused by the first lieutenant, who said, —

"If you want to witness a strange custom, come on deck: the Ainos are welcoming a chief who has been absent from his tribe."

"Can my mother and sister see the ceremony?" inquired Johnnie.

"Certainly," replied their friend. "You had better be quick."

The boys hastily put on their *kimono*, and on reaching the deck beheld a strange sight. Seven Ainos were dancing and shouting on the beach, and were brandishing their swords in a very threatening manner.

"They are full of fight," said Fitz.

"No, indeed," replied Sallie. "The captain says that is their way of saluting a distinguished person. Do you see the chief over there in the boat?"

The boys glanced in the indicated direction, and beheld two native craft, in the nearer of which a grave-looking man was seated behind a low screen that rose about a foot above the gunwale. The Ainos who accompanied him flourished their

weapons, and shouted back as though in defiance; and the rowers paddled with one hand, and gesticulated with the other.

Instead of landing opposite the ship, the chief ordered his people to row him round the point.

"They are very timid," said the first lieutenant. "I have seen a good deal of them, but often found great difficulty in inducing them to perform their rites in my presence. The farther you get into the interior, the more unsophisticated and gentle they are."

The Ainos on the shore danced out of sight, and those in the boats rowed as though anxious to hide from the foreigners' gaze.

"I call that a shame," said Sallie. "We would not have done them any harm by looking at the ceremony."

"They have a perfect right to do as they please," said practical Johnnie, who was watching some gulls through a telescope. "Hallo! what is that on the water?"

"A sleeping seal," replied the officer. "It will not be many moments before you see an Aino put out and capture him. That kind of seal is called *wuneo*. The gulls like to swim round it, I suppose on account of the little fishes, that, strangely enough, accompany the large one."

"The seal's eyes are open," remarked Fitz.

"Yes, but it is fast asleep," said the officer, bringing his telescope to bear upon the creature. "True, it moves its tail; but, without doubt, it is not awake."

"Hallo! here comes a boat," cried Fitz, as a canoe was rowed swiftly round the point. "How did they know about the fish?"

"There are a hundred pairs of Aino eyes watching from the beach," said the lieutenant. "The Yezo-jin have a strange

superstition. During the fishing-season the fishermen drink
no *saké*, keep their boats very clean, and worship the sea-god
and god of vessels by offering them *saké* and *inaho*. When
they start out to hunt the seal, they row very quietly ; while the
wife and children at home sit perfectly still, and do not make
the usual noise when eating, in order not to scare the game."

"Look at them," said Sallie : "one has laid down his paddles, and is standing up in the bow, balancing a double-headed
harpoon with a line attached to it."

SLEEPING SEAL.

By that time every one on board was watching the hunters,
who, quite unconscious of the interest they were exciting, had
approached to within sixty feet of their prey.

The harpooner stood quite motionless, leaving his companions to manage the craft. Suddenly he launched his weapon,
then grasped the line with both hands. The spear quivered as
it darted towards the seal, which it struck and awoke. In
another instant the fish sounded, — i. e., dived to the bottom, —
and the Aino hauled in the shaft of his harpoon.

"The barbed points are broken off," said Johnnie. "He
has lost his prize."

"Indeed he has not," answered the lieutenant. "The bone heads are poisoned, and are buried deeply in the body of the *wunco*. In a few moments the creature, thoroughly paralyzed, will float to the surface. They will have a great feast over their capture."

His information proved to be correct, though it was half an hour before the fish was secured.

The Ainos made a tremendous fuss over landing the seal, and welcomed the harpooner with joyful howls.

SPEARING A SEAL.

"I think we had better disembark," said the Professor. "It is nearly eight o'clock."

"You must breakfast first," said Capt. Imadate, who overheard the remark. "Will you please come down to the cabin? every thing is ready."

About nine o'clock they entered the commander's gig, and were rowed to the beach, upon which some Japanese and Ainos, who had been out fishing for menhaden, were landing their spoils, and were shouting and laughing, like a lot of school-boys, as they drew in the net, and deposited it upon mats spread on the sand.

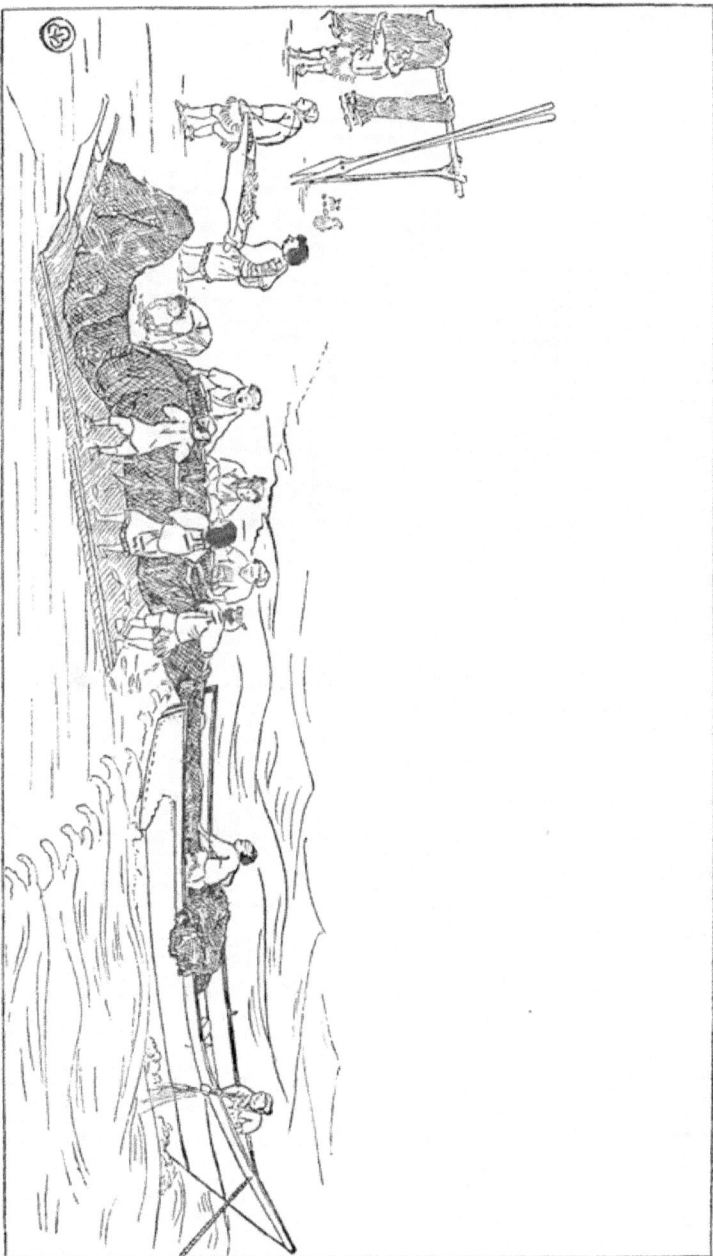

MENHADEN-FISHING.

" Why, they use handbarrows just like our Gloucester fisher-men, and hang their nets on racks," remarked Sallie.

" They know their business," said the Professor. " The party appear to have had very good luck. I should calculate there are several million of fish in that net. What do you say, Fitz ? "

" I have not brought my *soro-ban* " (counting-board), " sir," demurely an-swered the boy. " Never was good at guessing numbers."

His father frowned and said, " Do not be frivolous. Estimate the length and breadth of the net, the proportion of one of the fishes to the average height of the mass "— Then he suddenly stopped, and regarded an Aino, who had approached unob-served, and who looked as though he had an important communication to make.

"PLEASE GIVE TWO SHEWS."

The savage saluted by extending his hands and waving them inward ; after which he said, pointing his forefinger at the Professor, —

" Cappin, please — give two shews."

" Oh ! you speak English, do you, my friend ? " blandly answered the Professor. " I was not aware that you wore shoes."

Fitz chuckled, and whispered, —

" He does not want shoes, sir. He is evidently tobacco-hunting. Don't you understand? he wants two chews, — one for himself and the other for his chief."

The Aino's nostrils distended, the corners of his mouth

curved upwards, and he smiled like the end man of a minstrel troupe.

"Where is our interpreter?" asked the Professor, who was most anxious to improve the occasion. "I wish to explain to this poor creature the injurious effects of nicotine upon the system. The governor of Hakodate promised we should be met here by some one who could talk the Aino language."

Oto spoke to a custom-house officer who was inspecting their baggage, and the official replied by shouting to a group of females, —

"Habo-obari, come here!"

Upon hearing this, a young woman advanced toward the foreigners, and, kneeling upon the sand, bowed respectfully.

"She can speak Japanese," said the man, "and will accompany you into the interior;" adding, "Rise, Habo, and answer questions."

The woman, who was very gentle, sat up on her heels, and murmured in Japanese, "I am much ashamed. I know so little, but shall be very happy to do any thing for you."

The young Americans were delighted to be able to talk with her: so while the official was

"OUR INTERPRETER."

putting the custom-house mark on their baggage, they plied Habo with questions, and soon learned something of her history. She said, "I was taught by a Japanese lady in Hakodate, and would have remained there until now; but my parents wanted me to marry a chief, so I came home again."

" What is the matter with your mouth ? " said Mrs. Jewett.

" I have been tattooed," she replied : " that is the custom of our people."

" How is it done ? " inquired Sallie, regarding her pityingly.

" My mother scratched the lines round my mouth with a knife, and rubbed soot into them : then the marks were washed with an infusion of the bark of a tree, which made them blue. My hands are ornamented in the same way."

" Did it not hurt you ? " inquired the young lady.

TATTOOING ON AINO WOMAN'S HAND.

" Not much," she replied, drawing up the sleeve of her *kimono*, and exhibiting her arm : " my decoration is not all finished. Every Aino woman has this adornment."

" Well," murmured Fitz, speaking in English, and critically inspecting the lines, " I should call it a disfigurement."

Habo took a great liking to Sallie, and, in order to show her good-will, offered to tattoo her mouth.

" No, thank you," answered the young lady. " I am much obliged to you, all the same."

After a while Capt. Imadate, who had been detained on board the ship, joined them, and said, —

" I cannot understand how it is the officials from Kawanishi are not here to receive you. I will despatch a messenger
to ascertain the cause of their non-appearance."

While he was speaking, two Japanese officers, dressed in dark
blue uniforms, rode over the ridge, and approached the visitors.

After dismounting they saluted, and said, —

" We are instructed to receive a foreign professor and his
family, and to conduct them to Kawanishi. Are you the gentleman ? "

Professor Jewett answered in the affirmative : then he was
informed that ponies were on their way for the use of his party,
and that accommodation had been prepared for them at
Kawanishi.

The animals appeared about ten o'clock ; and with them
came sixty Ainos, some of whom were as hairy as bears.
These, of course, excited the boys' curiosity ; and they asked a
hundred questions through Habo, who said, —

" They never feel the cold, and live to be very aged. Some
Ainos have only a little hair on their necks, arms, and chests :
others are covered with it like a garment. We consider such
a growth to be very beautiful."

" There is no accounting for taste," said Fitz. " Why,"
nodding at the old fellow who had begged for tobacco, " here
is Deacon Andrews. Father never delivered that lecture on the
injurious effects of nicotine. Ask the gentleman why he waits
round here."

The woman spoke to the man, then replied to Fitz, —

" He says he is from your honorable country. He is a bad
person."

" Does he mean to assert that he is an American ? " queried
the boy.

"He was taken from Hakodate a long distance across the
sea," said Habo; "and he remained away until he was almost
forgotten. Since his return he has generally been in prison.
People said that he acquired vicious habits in the foreign
country. No one knows where he went or how he earned his
living."

"I guess he went to New York, and ran for alderman,"
gravely answered Johnnie. "He has a hungry, unsatisfied look.
Tell him that none of us use tobacco in any form."

"Come, Sallie, here is your pony," said the Professor:
"you will have to hold on, for there is no side-saddle. Fitz,
you take the black one; and Johnnie the piebald, next to him."

They said *saïonara* (farewell) to the captain, then, mounting
their steeds, rode up the sand-ridge, and found themselves in
a swampy tract, entirely destitute of roads, which necessitated
the party's proceeding in Indian file.

The officers from Kawanishi acted as their guides; and the
Ainos led the ponies, and kept them at a trot.

Towards evening they forded a river, and began to ascend
the mountains.

At sunset they reached a government establishment where
their servants were enabled to prepare supper in American
fashion.

"There are lots of Ainos in this place," remarked Oto.
"The officers from Kawanishi have gone to see the chief of
the tribe who inhabit this district. If you like, we will drop in
upon them later in the evening."

"Certainly," said the Professor. "Hark to the sound of
that musical instrument! I believe the natives are giving a
concert."

When supper was over, Professor Jewett, Fitz, Johnnie, and

Oto quitted the house, leaving Mrs. Jewett and Sallie to talk with Habo.

" Yonder are the officers," said Johnnie, pointing to an Aino hut. " Let us look in at the window, and watch them."

" That would offend the Yezo-jin," said Oto. " They never do such a thing, or throw refuse out of a window. You must respect their superstitions."

" Please come in," said one of the officers. " This chief is very anxious to entertain you."

AINO HUT.

The party entered, and beheld eight Ainos, seated on new mats that had been spread upon the ground in honor of their guests, who, in the absence of chairs, had been accommodated with blocks of wood.

Five lacquer boxes, containing food, were placed upon the floor; and a woman, whose head was tied with a white fillet, was pouring out *saké* from a long-handled *nagaye* (ladle).

The chief requested the Americans to join his guests, so the Professor said, —

" Let us seat ourselves on this heap of mats, and watch the

proceedings. I suppose this is what the natives consider an aristocratic gathering."

When they were accommodated, and the lacquer cups had been filled with *saké*, the Ainos raised their vessels, which they waved towards them three times, then took their carved *saké*-sticks, dipped them in the wine, and made formal libations to the *inaho*. They lifted their mustaches with the sticks, so as

AINOS ENTERTAINING JAPANESE OFFICIALS.

not to saturate them with the *saké*, and drained the cups with a sucking noise, considered by them to be the height of politeness. The Ainos did not content themselves with a single cup, but drank a great number in rapid succession.

In vain the Japanese officials endeavored to keep up with their entertainers; for, though intellectually by far their superiors, they lacked the muscular vigor and strong heads of the savages, and were soon compelled to set down their cups untasted.

The chief made his graceful salutation, then said, —

" My old grandfather will sing, and play on the *ka*."

A woman then entered, carrying a musical instrument about four feet in length, which was passed round for the inspection of the foreigners. It had five strings, made from the fibre of a plant called *mosha-kina*, and a bridge of whale-tooth ivory.

" It looks as though it had been whittled out with a jack-knife," said Fitz. " I suppose they think it a wonderful piece of workmanship. It is heavy enough for a war-club."

" The decoration is severely simple," remarked his father. " These archaic forms are most interesting. Evidently the *ka* is of very ancient origin, all pictures of primitive musical instruments being long and narrow. I wonder whether the chief would sell this."

MOSHA-KINA.

Upon his speech being interpreted to their host, the latter replied, —

" It is the property of my grandfather: he would not part with it for any money. Here he comes."

As he spoke an old Aino entered the hut, saluted every one gracefully, and, after he had been served with *saké*, took the *ka*,

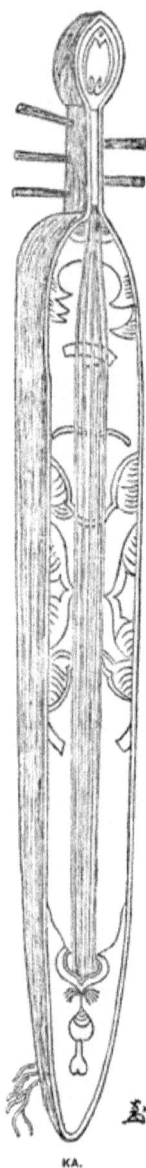

and began to play a weird air in a minor key. At intervals he would open his mouth, and utter a curious noise which began like the howling of a dog, and ended with a sharp barking note.

"We had a puppy that used to sing like that," said the mirth-loving Fitz. "He always performed when Sallie practised on the piano."

Oto smiled, and replied in Japanese, —

"These Ainos are remarkably like dogs."

"Dogs are very good creatures, after all," said Johnnie; adding, "Upon what are we sitting?"

Oto lifted the mat, and found that they had been resting upon the body of the seal they had seen caught by the Ainos. The fish had been dressed, and prepared for transport by securing its fins to its tail, so as to form a loop through which a pole could be passed to carry it.

The chief explained that the *wunco* was in his charge to forward into the interior.

"Oh! he runs an express-office," said Fitz. "I hope we have not damaged the package."

When this was translated to the Aino, he replied, —

"My storehouse was burned down yesterday; and I was afraid the rats would get at the

seal, so I brought it indoors. I think it is very probable you will eat some of the delicious flesh, as it is going to the chief at Kawanishi."

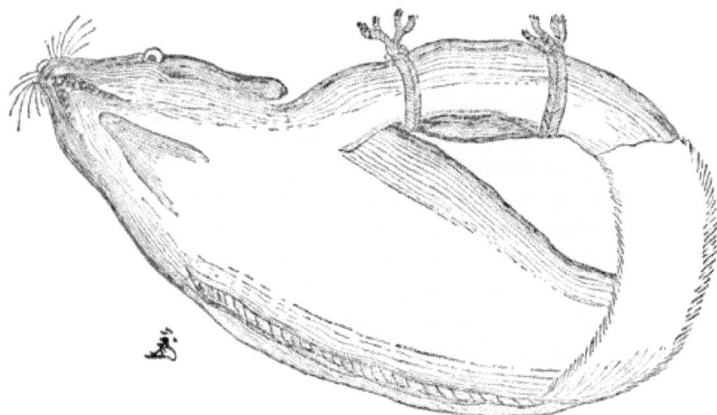

SEAL PREPARED FOR TRANSPORTATION.

"Not if I know myself," murmured Fitz. "I shall have to be very hungry before I partake of it."

"Come, boys," said the Professor, "it is time we returned to our hotel. Your mother and sister will be anxious about us."

The Ainos rose, and conducted their guests to the door ; and, as the foreigners took their leave, the savages made their graceful salutation, and cried, —

"*Saramba ! Saram-ba !*" (good-by).

AINO STOREHOUSE

"What is that light flashing to the northward?" inquired Johnnie.

"It is from a burning mountain," answered Oto. "Yezo is

famous for its volcanoes. You will see several active ones during your journey."

They found Mrs. Jewett and Sallie fast asleep, and Habo watching them like a faithful animal.

CHAPTER IV.

KAWANISHI.

" Confucius said, ·Within the four seas, all men are brothers ;` notwithstanding which, one does not care to acknowledge the Aino as a relative."

THE travellers rose very early, and started amid the saluta-
tions and murmured " *saramba* " of the Ainos.

" There is the *wunco* we are to have for dinner to-day," said
Johnnie, pointing to the seal, that, slung on a pole, was carried
by two sturdy savages. " Come along, Sallie : I will race you
for a dollar."

" No, thank you," replied his sister. " The road is not wide
enough for that sort of amusement."

As the party progressed, they became soaked through with
the drippings from the trees, and the tall bamboo grass that
overhung the path. On either side the forest was a wall of
herbage, knitted together with enormous trailing plants, inter-
spersed with gigantic *beckonoshita* (dock), some of the stems of
which were eight feet high, and had leaves two yards in di-
ameter.

In one spot was a clearing in which stood an Aino man and
two women, one of the latter bashfully hiding herself beneath
a leaf that covered her like an extinguisher.

" This plant is called the *nadosmia Japonica*," said Professor Jewett, reining in his pony ; " and I should think it is the
largest of its species."

" Please go on, husband," said his wife. " The soakage

from the trees has chilled me.   I shall be glad when we arrive
at our destination."

"I do not call this a road," grumbled Johnnie.

BECKONOSHITA (GIGANTIC DOCK).

"No, it is a dog's track in a howling wilderness," cried the
merry Fitz. "I have all sorts of insects in my clothes; and

some of them nip, I tell you. One cannot expect macadamized roads and Pullman cars in Yezo."

"That is true," cheerfully responded Sallie. "Remember, we promised papa, that, come what might, we would not grumble."

They halted at a place called Holaiku-kotan, a mere collection of huts in a clearing, where they were welcomed by a venerable savage, who was said to be a hundred years old. As no one seemed to know his name, the boys addressed him as "Uncle Remus," which appeared to do just as well as any other.

"How he chuckles!" said Fitz. "One would think he understood all we said. I wonder whether he ever took a bath."

Habo was summoned; and soon the patriarch showed, that, though the frosts of many winters had whitened his hair, his intelligence, what there was of it, was unimpaired. He said that he was very poor, and would have no objection to taste a little *saké*. In the absence of wine, Fitz mixed him a draught of Jamaica-ginger and water; which the old boy pronounced *pirika* (good), and in return offered the young Americans some liquor made from the root of a tree. Upon their declining his gift, he drained the contents of the bowl, wiped his mouth with the back of his hand, and remarked,—

"It is all the same: I have drunk for you, and you will get the benefit."

By this he meant that the gods would accept it as an offering.

When they parted from him, he chuckled worse than ever, and, leaning on his staff and against the door of his hut, watched them until they were out of sight.

The sun had dried the undergrowth, and rendered the atmosphere as hot and moist as that of a forcing-house for plants: travelling was therefore fatiguing, and the Americans. were heartily glad when they arrived at Kawanishi, where they found quite a settlement of Japanese and Ainos.

UNCLE REMUS.
[FROM PHOTOGRAPH LOANED BY PROF. MUNROE.]

They were welcomed by the assistant governor of the Ken, who proved to be an old friend of Oto's.

After enjoying the luxury of a warm bath, they dined, then accompanied their host into the kitchen, where they found Aino servants preparing food for the various officials of the establishment.

"You see," said their host, "we have trained the natives to

cook in Japanese style, and they are really quite expert at it.
That big iron pot is suspended over the fire in Aino fashion,
otherwise every thing is Japanese. Yonder is the chief cook,
who is handing a bowl of rice to my interpreter. The man
behind him is stirring grated fish and bean-flour into a paste,
and the woman at the back is washing the roe of a *koi* in a

JAPANESE KITCHEN AT KAWANISHI.

sieve. The women on the left are sorting rice, which that hairy
Aino is hulling. He is what we term in Japan a *kome-tsuki*, and
is a very powerful fellow. Another servant has just taken some
dried salmon from a bale of the fish. He will cut it into shreds,
and serve it to the servants with their rice. You observe that
Aino in the back kitchen: he is feeding the furnace under a
boiler in which we steam cakes. That dog is a very good one
to keep watch: he never allows any strange Aino to enter the

premises. All our servants have adopted the Japanese custom of taking hot baths, and are very faithful and honest."

The officer evidently liked the natives, and was well posted with regard to their manners and customs. He conducted his guests into the reception-room, where they saw several pictures depicting scenes of Aino life.

"This," he said, indicating a painting representing a *daimio* (great lord) entertaining four Yezo-jin, "represents a very curious incident. The Ainos had been somewhat unruly, and had not paid tribute to the lord of Matsumai. Instead of punishing them, he inquired what kind of food they liked best ; and was informed that they greatly esteemed a sort of cake made of sea-weed, venison, ground millet, and dried *koi* cooked in whale-oil."

"Sort of Yezo fish-ball," suggested Fitz.

"Yes," answered their host. "The *daimio* told his chief counsellor to have a number of these prepared, and to summon the disaffected chiefs. Matsumai received them seated behind a curtain bearing his crest, three diamonds forming a lozenge. When the *zen* (trays) were brought in, the chief counsellor said, —

"'Your lord bids you eat with him.'

"Upon the Ainos discovering that the noble condescended to partake of their favorite dish, they stroked their beards, and exclaimed, —

"'*Pirika !*' (good), 'great is the condescension of our lord : after this we consider ourselves like the sand beneath his feet.'"

"Well, it is an interesting picture," said Fitz ; "and the old Ainos appear to be tickled to death. But the *daimio* does not seem to relish the mess : he looks like one of our ward politicians at a cheap dinner given to his followers."

LORD OF MATSUMAI AND THE AINOS.

"What does this second picture represent?" inquired Sallie. "Are not those ships meant for foreign men-of-war?"

"The hull of the nearest one appears to be built of bricks," said Fitz.

"That is an historical scene," answered the officer. "During the Japanese period of Kwan-sei (A. D. 1789), some Russian ships appeared off this island, and caused great consternation among the natives, who feared they were about to be seized, and carried into slavery. When the foreigners landed, the Ainos attacked them with bows and arrows; whereupon the Russians retreated to their vessels, and have never returned. They were evidently afraid of the Yezo-jin."

"I do not believe it was that," said Johnnie. "I believe the Ainos mistook a party landing in search of water, for invaders; and that there is more fighting in this picture than there was in reality."

"What is this third scene?" asked Sallie.

"That depicts the annual distribution of allowances to the Yezo-jin in the olden time. The Ainos then belonged to the *daimios* of their provinces, and half of the bear and other skins they procured in hunting were paid as tribute to their lords. In return for this, they received protection, and once a year were given allowances of rice, tobacco, and *saké*, which were regulated according to the offerings made by each chief. On the appointed day they had audience with the representative of their *daimio*, who was accompanied by six witnesses from the Shogun's government, two interpreters, and a number of retainers of the lord of Matsumai, who saw that each chief received his allowance.

"The official seated himself on a mat inside the house, his secretary knelt upon his left, the witnesses ranged themselves

INVASION OF YEZO BY THE RUSSIANS, A.D. 1789.

against the wall, and the interpreters took up their positions on the boarded space in front of the edifice.   Then the Ainos advanced, and knelt upon mats they had brought with them ; the four principal chiefs being in the front row, and the others according to their rank."

" Those are the head chiefs in the decorative-art *kimono*, are they not?" said Sallie.

DISTRIBUTING ALLOWANCES TO AINOS.

The officer smiled, and continued, —

" After the Ainos had saluted, the secretary took a document from a *sambo* upon his right, and proceeded to read the list of awards in this manner : —

" ' Ipocash-ku, two hundred skins; two bales of rice, one tub of *saké*, and two bundles of tobacco.

" ' Kanta-chip, one hundred and fifty skins; one bale of rice, one tub of *saké*, and one bundle of tobacco.'

"Each announcement was translated to the Ainos, who saluted and howled by way of approval.

"When the ceremony was over, they retired to their homes, and, seating themselves upon new mats, drank to the gods and their lord; generally finishing up with a *tai-fu-kari*, or bird-dance. Here," producing a book, "is a representation of the ceremony."

TAI-FU-KARI DANCE.

"There are four ladies engaged in the amusement," remarked Johnnie. "Do they indulge in *saké*?"

"Yes," said their host. "The Aino women drink as much as the men. They serve the wine, and always secure their share."

"Please tell us about the dance," said Sallie, who was anxious to learn the manners and customs of the Yezo-jin.

"The vessel filled with *saké* is placed on a clean mat, two cups on rests and sticks being set before it. Then the Ainos squat round and drink until they feel in the humor to dance, when they rise, clap their hands, and begin to sing, —

> ' I am a bird, and can fly
> Over the river and fire :
> I am a god.'

" They caper round and round, flap their arms as a crow does its wings, and imitate the birds ; until, overcome by the violent exercise and the *saké*, they fall down and go to sleep."

" How degraded they are ! " said Sallie. " I think they ought to be taught better."

" I reckon a good many of our people are very much like them," said Fitz. " Their dances appear to be harmless."

" Yes," said Oto : " they are not, like some foreigners, in the habit of shooting one another by way of a climax to their amusement."

That evening they went to see Habo's father, whom they found busily engaged whittling out *inaho* (god-sticks). He was crouching by the side of his hut, against which rested his bows ; and he had a sword, and a box of arrow-poison, on the ground near him.

Habo saluted him respectfully ; but he did not condescend to reply, or to take any notice of his American visitors.

" He does not seem well to-day," she whispered. " He is very old, and has pains in his bones which spoil his temper. When he feels very badly, he makes *inaho*, which occupation generally cures him.   The bear-skin he wears came from a *hokuyak* he killed two winters ago."

" I suppose he is too sick even to drink *saké ?* " mischievously remarked Fitz.

The old fellow's eyes twinkled ; and, guessing what was said, he ceased his occupation, and saluted his visitors, saying, —

"I always feel better after I have emptied a cup."

Habo went to a neighboring house, and returned with a bowl of the coveted liquid, which her father absorbed without so much as winking.

Poor Habo meekly received the cup, and turning to Mrs. Jewett, gently remarked, —

"As men grow old, their bodies become like dried wood, and they require liquid nourishment. A few years ago my father was a great chief: now he has re- tired, and only thinks of making *inaho*."

"I think he need not be so grumpy," said Fitz in English. "My opinion is, his daughter is too kind to him."

The old man's red eyes flashed, though he did not understand the words: then he

HABO'S FATHER.

once more doubled himself up, grasped his knife, and resumed his whittling.

"What a sad spectacle!" mused the Professor. "And that is a man!"

"No, sir," said Oto : "he is the missing link between man and the monkey. I have, in other countries beside Yezo, seen creatures that resembled him."

Habo next introduced her friends to her mother, who was, if possible, more weird-looking than the old chief. She was busily

employed pounding millet in a wooden mortar, and, consid-
ering her fragile appearance, performed her task with considerable vim. She listened to her daughter in grim silence,
then continued her occupation without condescending to
reply.

"Mother is very busy," said Habo. "If she does not have
the food ready at the proper time, father will feel sad."

"She means get mad," said Fitz in English. "You may
depend upon it, that old
savage has made his wife's
existence a burden to
her." On their return to
the assistant governor's
house they were met by
their host, who said, —

"The chief has de-
termined to perform the
ceremony of *oukari*.
Would you like to wit-
ness it?"

WOODEN PESTLE AND MORTAR.

"By all means," answered the Professor. "Can the ladies
be present?"

Their friend thought not; remarking, —

"It is really a trial of endurance, and sometimes the Ainos
have been known to die under it. It is similar to the *oukari*,
their most severe form of punishment, combined with a spas-
modic generosity that causes the entertainer to give away his
treasures in a most foolish manner. The chief, whom you met
last night, has invited you to be his guests: so you must not
be offended if he gives you presents."

After dinner the Professor and his sons accompanied

Oto and the official to the spot set apart for the ceremony, — a rough piece of pasture-land on the bank of a river.

They were received very politely, and, having taken their places on some bales of fish covered with mats, were offered *saké* in the usual manner.

Habo, who was present, acted as interpreter; and through her the chief said, —

" *Oukari* is a very ancient custom, and is intended to try the courage of our people. I shall give a reward to all who can bear the punishment like men;" then, addressing his wife, he added, " Bring in the club."

The woman went to a neighboring hut, through the window of which a weapon was passed with great ceremony. It was of hard wood, about forty-five inches long, and in shape very much like what we term an Indian club.

She carried it very respectfully, and handed it to a bearded Aino; who, before receiving it, spat on his hands like a boy about to use a base-ball bat. At this stage of the proceedings, a muscular Yezo-jin, who wore across his shoulders a mat made of sealskins, joined the party, and, solemnly saluting the chief, took up his place before him.

The women arranged the mat so that it completely protected the wearer from the waist to the nape of the neck; he holding the ends of the covering in his outstretched hands.

Fitz's eyes twinkled; and he whispered to his father, —

" This is going to be a lark."

" You mean that the rite will prove interesting," said his parent. " I do not quite understand the use of that mass of sealskin."

" Guess it is for the same purpose as I used to wear a

book under my jacket when I expected trouble at school," said
Fitz. " These Ainos act very much like children."

Two men then seated themselves as umpires for the club-
bearer, and the same number stood up and acted as friends
of the gentleman in the sealskin sack.

" Now the ceremony is going to begin," said Habo.   •

Saké was served ; after which the man with the mat braced
himself, and the one with the club swung it like a professional

OUKARI

gymnast, and brought it to bear with terrific force upon the
sealskins.

" *Shne* " (one), piped an old Aino, whose duty it was to
count the blows. He was very much bent, and what hair
remained seemed to be slipping off the back of his head.

" *Tu* " (two), " *re* " (three), " *ine* " (four), " *asne* " (five),
" *iwambe* " (six), " *aruwambe* " (seven), " *tupesambe* " (eight),
" *shnepesnabe* " (nine), " *wambi* " (ten). As each number was
called, the club descended, whack ! and the man holding the
mat staggered beneath the blows.

When *hots* (twenty) was called, the Ainos stopped the cere-

mony, and refreshed themselves with *saké;* after which the
amusement proceeded.

"I should think the blows would injure the spine," remarked the Pròfessor. " How many can they bear, Habo?"

"Sometimes *asne-hots*" (one hundred), she replied: " however, that is only in the case of a very strong man. This one
will not take more than *wambi-i-tuhots*" (fifty).

The amusement was suddenly interrupted by an accident
that threatened to terminate fatally. The club-swinger was
raising his weapon in order to deal the thirty-seventh blow,
when a hornet stung him on the wrist and caused him to deliver
a foul ; the weapon slanting upwards, and striking his victim a
tremendous blow on the back of the skull.

At first the spectators thought he was dead ; but Oto examined him, and said, —

"If you keep him quiet, he will come round after a while.
Any one but a Yezo-jin would have been kil'ed· by such a
blow." When the chief learned the doctor's decision, he
said, —

" Hokutakane shall have two fishes, and two bales of goods.
He has shown that he can take punishment like an Aino."

More *saké* was served, and another Aino was soon found to
shoulder the sealskin pad.

The second man succumbed at the twentieth stroke ; and
the third cried, "Hold!" before he had received the fifth,
Habo explaining that he was not very well.

"I should not think he would feel so now," said Johnnie.
" I tell you, one blow from that weapon would disarrange my
anatomical system."

About twenty men had their powers of endurance tested,
and received presents varying from a dried salmon to two bales

of goods. When the last stroke was delivered, the chief arose a poor man; and his friends had more or less sore backs, and proportionate proofs of his generosity.

Although the foreigners did not submit to the ordeal, they each received presents; the Professor's share being an antique Owari jar, decorated under the glaze with curious crossed lines in pipe-clay. It had been used for storing *saké*, and bore marks of having been set upon the fire.

"It will please Sallie," said Fitz. "She likes old crockery of this description. When she sees it she will say, 'It is too sweet for any thing.'"

The *oukari* wound up with a grand *taifu-kari*, in which all the contestants danced; even the man who had been

OWARI JAR.

rendered senseless having recovered sufficiently to take part in the final exercise.

The performers waved their arms, cawed like crows, shouted, hopped first on one leg and then on the other, and barked like dogs; even the children capering in the same fashion. Then a big mess of food was brought in a lacquered box bearing a *tomoye* (luck-mark), three *inaho* were driven in the ground, and the chief's wives ladled out this strange-looking mass.

"Come," said the Professor, "let us retire: to-morrow we shall start for the wilds of Yezo."

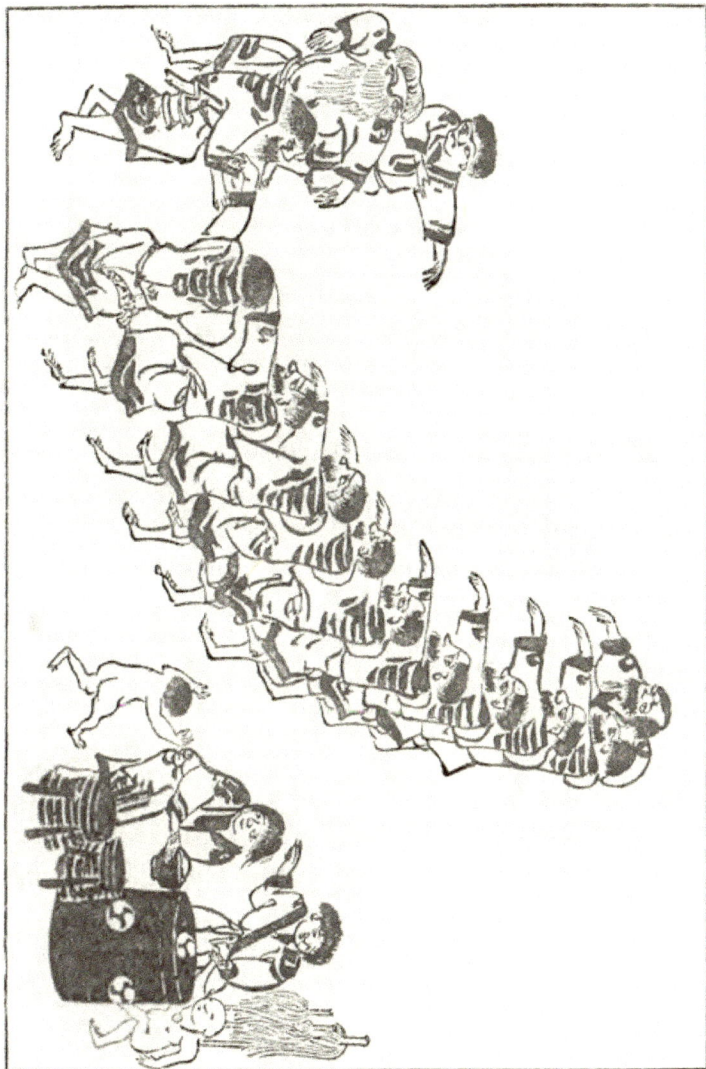

WINDING UP THE EVENING'S ENTERTAINMENT.

CHAPTER V.

IN THE MOUNTAINS OF YEZO.

"The Japanese say, 'Travelling is an inch of purgatory.' The Ainos have an adage which translates thus: 'At home you can be happy; but when you go upon a journey, you enjoy four periods of misery to one of pleasure.'"

"COME, young folks," said the Professor, "make your toilets. It is a long journey between here and Hokuyakbets; and you will have to walk, or be carried by the Ainos. Habo says the horses cannot climb the mountain passes."

Fitz rubbed his eyes, and drowsily replied, —

"I never knew any good result from rising early. It disarranges a poor little fellow for the entire day. Why not start at ten o'clock, and take it easy?"

"Oh, you lazy boy!" said Sallie. "I have been up an hour. Habo tells me we are going through some very delightful scenery, and that it is worth a great deal to see the sun rise over the mountains. Don't keep us waiting: I have made some delicious coffee for you."

"That will be an inducement," said her sleepy brother. "Count me in for two cups, Sallie. I won't keep you a minute. What time is it?"

"Just half-past three," she replied.

As Fitz donned his clothes, he grumbled, —

"I do not see much use going to bed when one has to get up at this unearthly hour. Well, I suppose it is an Aino custom."

"That settles it," said Fitz; adding, with a significant gesture to the woman, "Suppose he has no child?"

Habo thought a while, then replied, —

"He will adopt one: it would be just the same, according to Aino ideas."

While they were talking, the young merchant had been making a sketch, which he handed to Sallie, saying, —

"Please accept this little picture to remind you of the story related by your interpreter. My father has a very fine painting representing the scene. He was one of the retainers of the lord of Matsumai."

Sallie thanked him, and the party resumed their journey.

That night they slept in an old *hon-jin ;* i.e., a house formerly used by the *daimios* and their trains.

It was in a very dilapidated state, and, though long since abandoned by man, was well tenanted with very lively insects.

"What species do you call these, papa?" said Fitz, as he rose and met his father, who had been fairly driven into the open air.

"The *pulex horridus,*" savagely returned the Professor. "They are the most insatiate creatures I have ever encountered. Travelling among the Ainos is not unalloyed pleasure."

"Particularly when you have to rise soon after retiring, in order to accommodate the permanent boarders," was the merry response. "I believe they look upon Johnnie as a public benefactor, or he must have taken a sleeping draught."

"Not a bit of it," wearily ejaculated his brother, emerging slowly from the house. "I have lost pounds of flesh. I do not think they have left any thing of mother and Sallie."

While they were chatting, Habo came from an adjoining building, and on seeing them inquired what was the matter.

Upon being informed, she expressed great astonishment, and naïvely remarked, —

" No Aino minds those little *taiki*. We should feel lonely without them."

" They are sociable enough," growled Johnnie. " If you like them so much, why are you not enjoying their society ? "

The woman simpered, then replied, —

" There is to be a *machi-koro*" (wedding) " at midnight. The son of the Aino who looks after this *hon-jin* is to be married to a very pretty girl named Kisara."

" Can we witness the ceremony ? " asked the Professor.

At first Habo looked serious : however, she finally said, —

" I think they will not mind, because you are very gentle, and do not laugh at our customs. I will go and ask if they will object to your presence."

She re-entered the building, and, after remaining absent a while, returned, saluted, and said, —

" The father of the boy says you are welcome to see his son married, but fears you will feel very much amused at the cere-mony. We are an ignorant people, and this man is very poor. Please follow me, and kindly avoid speaking."

She led the way ; and the Americans presently found them-selves in an octagonal room, built in Japanese fashion, and floored with reed mats. This had formerly been a reception-hall, but was now used by the Aino janitor and his family.

In the centre was a fireplace, a frame of wood filled with ashes, on which were a pile of chips and some sticks of res-inous pine. The usual kettle hung over the pile; and a lamp formed of a large shell rested on a little post at one corner of the fireplace, which was decorated with three *inaho* (god-sticks).

The bridegroom's father saluted his foreign guests, and said he was very much honored by their presence.

" This is to be a dark _séance_," said the fun-loving Fitz.

" Hush, hush ! " cautioned his father.   " Seat yourself here, and keep quiet.   I consider it a very great privilege to be present on such an interesting occasion."

There was a glimmer of light among the kindling on the hearth; and they could just discern the outlines of their host and his son, who seated themselves on the left of the frame.

Habo crouched near the Americans, and, in a low voice, explained what was being done.

" Only the family and certain friends are present," she said. " The middle-man, who has arranged the marriage, will bring in the bride, who is supposed to be invisible."

" I should think she is," said Fitz.   " I do not believe a cat could see its kitten by this light."

After a brief interval they heard a rustling noise, and then dimly beheld a bearded Aino, followed by a dark figure, who, as she entered the apartment, knelt behind her conductor.   The latter bowed, and, saluting the father of the bridegroom, said,—

" Is your son lonely ? "

" Yes," replied the old man.   " He is very lonely indeed."

No more was said, the bridegroom remaining perfectly motionless, while the go-between retired; leaving the girl, who approached the fireplace, and taking a resinous chip pushed it into the embers.

Presently the flame blazed up, and revealed her face, which was really a pretty one.

She lighted the lamp, then bowed, and remained with her face hidden from view.

The bridegroom rose, and, approaching his bride, led her

to his father. Then the pair bowed, the young wife stirred
up the fire, and the family welcomed her with murmurs of
approbation.

"That is all," said Habo. "Now everybody leaves, and
goes to the young folks' house to drink *saké.*"

The foreign visitors took the hint, and retired.

MACHI-KORO (AINO MARRIACE).

"Yours is a very simple ceremony, Habo," remarked the
Professor, seating himself in the veranda of the *hon-jin.* "How
old are the bride and groom?"

"The man is twenty-two, and the girl eighteen," she answered.

"Did he select her himself?" inquired Johnnie.

"Oh, yes!" replied Habo. "He has seen her many times,
and noticed that she could cook, split bark, cut wood, and do

hard work : so he made up his mind to marry her. Then he
went to the Japanese authorities and to his chief, and asked
permission to have the girl. When this was granted, he sought
out a friend of his family to act as go-between, and sent her
father a sword, lacquer cup, or curio, the acceptance of which
settled the matter."

"Why did the go-between bring the bride in in the dark?"
inquired Fitz.

"No one is supposed to know who she is," answered Habo.
"Women, being descendants of the goddess who founded our
race, are considered to be light-makers for the house, and to
render it bright and cheerful. Now will you come to their
home, and drink *saké*?"

"Please excuse us," said the Professor. "It does not agree
with me, and my sons never touch it. — Boys, what do you say?
shall we try once more to woo the drowsy god?"

"I cannot keep my eyes open any longer," said Fitz, "and
shall have to again brave the terrors of those old mats."

About eight o'clock the next morning they were awakened
by a commotion in the establishment, and, upon inquiring the
cause, were informed that the chief Setta-eye had arrived from
Hokuyak-bets to conduct them to his village.

"He is a very great man," said Habo; "and his wife is
exceedingly beautiful."

"We ought to receive him with some sort of ceremony,"
said the Professor. "Come, my sons, brush up a bit, and I will
tell your mother and sister of the honor awaiting us."

Just then Oto, who looked as though he had rested well,
joined them, and remarked, —

"I slept like a top. You boys look as though you had
been up all night."

" You must be iron-clad," said Johnnie. " I do not believe any of us has slept a wink."

" Why, what troubled you ? " inquired the doctor.

" I had about a million of them all at once," grumbled Fitz.

" Why did you not bring some insect-powder?" demanded their friend. " I thought you had laid in a stock. Well, I have enough for us all."

" I am thankful for that," ejaculated Mrs. Jewett. " I wonder we could have been so foolish as to forget ours. Poor Sallie is in a high state of fever."

" Wife," said the Professor, " Chief Setta-eye is anxious to have an interview with us. I do not wish to keep him waiting."

" He will have to wait until I make myself presentable," said the lady. " I want some water and a bowl."

Habo, who had listened attentively, hurried off, and soon returned with a lacquer cup holding about a quarter of a pint.

" I cannot wash in that," said Mrs. Jewett. " What do your people use ? "

" Nothing," was the *naïve* reply. " An Aino never puts water on his skin : it makes him sick."

" What ! You never take baths ? "

" Never," was the calm response.

" That settles it, mother," said Johnnie. " We shall have to buy a *saké*-tub, and carry it along with us, or dry-polish ourselves as the Ainos do."

After some delay the travellers accomplished their toilets, and Habo was informed that they would see their visitor.

In a few moments Setta-eye entered, and proved to be the finest Aino they had yet seen.

He extended his arms, waved his hands inward three times, then, stroking his superb beard, said in a dignified manner, —

" I have come to welcome you to my country."

He wore on his head a *sha-hobi* (a sort of crown), made of

CHIEF SETTA-EYE.

the fine bark of the tree from which they obtain the fibre for
their clothing; and suspended from his side was a Japanese

sword, handsomely mounted with gold. His dress was of bark cloth, trimmed with blue and white cotton : he carried an un-strung bow in his hand, and had large metal rings in his ears.

"What a magnificent savage!" murmured the Professor. "Look at his powerful physique, and see how hairy he is."

"Yes," answered Oto, "he is a good specimen of the Aino."

Setta-eye waited until they had ceased speaking, then said, in a gentle, musical tone, that contrasted strangely with his savage appearance, —

SHITOKI.

"I have been informed of your coming, and, knowing the road between here and Hokuyak-bets is dangerous, have brought my own people to guard you. Will you trust yourself to my poor care?"

"A thousand thanks," said the Professor. "We are indeed obliged for your thoughtfulness."

The chief then introduced his wife, who was dressed in a bark robe trimmed with blue cloth, confined at the waist by a narrow girdle. Her earrings were of silver, adorned with strips of red cotton tape; and she wore a *shitoki* (necklace of silver

and stone beads), to which was suspended an ornamental ring
of old-gold lacquer, decorated with a bamboo pattern.   Her

SETTA-EYE'S WIFE.

finger-nails were long and pointed, the tattooing about her
mouth and between her eyebrows was very fine and close, and
she carried a shuttle in her hand.

The *shitoki* is only worn by the wives of Aino chiefs, and is considered the most honorable distinction bestowed upon a woman.

Mrs. Jewett and Sallie, who looked red-eyed and sleepy, shook hands with the chief's wife, and asked her many questions about the road she had travelled. Her replies were made in a low, sweet voice; and, although she had never before seen foreigners, she bore herself with the greatest ease and dignity.

Setta-eye informed the Professor that he had prepared a habitation for him at Hokuyak-bets, and that he hoped he would remain some time his guest; adding,—

" I encountered several bears on my way hither : if you have any weapons with you, you had better put them in order."

" We have rifles," replied the Professor. " Hereto we have not met with any game, so I have forbidden my sons to carry arms. Now we will be prepared."

" 'Rah !" cried Fitz. " This is worth coming for. Now won't we have some fun ! If I come within range of a bear, I'll make him bite the dust."

CHAPTER VI.

AN AINO HOME.

" An exile from home, splendor dazzles in vain!
Oh, give me my lowly thatched cottage again!"

J. HOWARD PAYNE.

" My heart sinks within me when I no longer see my beloved home." — AINO
SONG.

NO civilized being is more devotedly attached to his home
than is the savage Aino, who, unlike other primitive
people, is not a nomad, and who can scarcely be induced to
quit his native place.

It was really touching to witness the joy of Setta-eye and his
wife when they once more beheld their hut.

"There is the *hokuyak*," cried the woman, pointing to a
bear, confined in a wooden cage. "See, he is sitting up to
welcome us."

"Look at those geese," cried Johnnie. "May I have a shot
at them, father?"

Setta-eye understood the question, and motioned the boy
to level his weapon. Johnnie did so, and succeeded in killing
two of the birds, which fell among the brushwood, and were
presently brought in by some Aino children.

The chief's house was a large structure, covered and
thatched with fine reeds, which were secured by slats tied to
the frame-work. The entrance was through a low archway, on
the floor of which was laid a new mat in honor of the visitors.

A rude fence of branches and stakes protected two sides of the edifice, and gave the place a very rustic look.

The chief, who was evidently respected by the people, invited his guests into his house, and assigned them places of honor on the benches occupying the left corner of the apartment.

When they had seated themselves he offered them *saké* and water; then retired, leaving them to rest, while he went to see if every thing was in order in the structure he had built for their accommodation.

"This is quite a nice place," said Johnnie. "They don't have much furniture, do they? I wonder what is in those bags up there."

"Those are skins of seals, sewn together, to contain the fish-oil used for light and cooking," said Habo. "This chief must be very wealthy to have so much oil in his house." She then told them the names of the various objects, saying, —

"We call the hearth *isumbé*. The fire-gods are *habaye-kamoi*, not *inaho*. That shell on a stick, used as a lamp, is the *nochi-beck;* the pot hanging from the roof is a *sho*. The quiver for arrows is called *ika*. The long sword is *tanephu*, and the short *emoshi*. That club is for *oukari*. Those lacquer boxes, *shin-toku ;* the bowl with four handles, *umpei;* the *saké*-kettle, *yehonitts ;* the chopsticks, *hekohasch ;* the *saké*-cup, *toki ;* the cup-stand, *takashiyate*. The square boxes are called *sheoff*."

"Now we know all about it," said Fitz, who had written down the names. "Why does that hooked pole hanging from the roof have an iron hoop at the bottom, and a piece of iron projecting from it?"

"The hoop is to suspend pots from," she answered; "and the piece of iron is used to swing them clear of the fire."

INTERIOR OF SETTA-EYE'S HUT.

" What is the curved piece of wood used for, that is lying on the mats near the fireplace ? " asked Johnnie.

" We put bear-meat on that to roast," she answered.   " You cannot take things off a very fierce fire with your fingers."

While they were conversing, Setta-eye entered, and, saluting, said, —

" Your home will soon be ready for your reception.   My

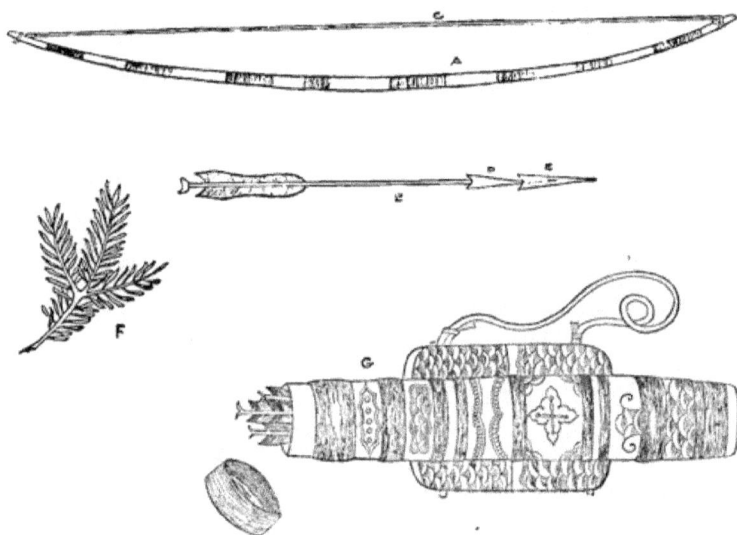

AINO WEAPONS.

wife is seeing that it is well smoked to drive out the mosquitoes."

When he took off his weapons, the young Americans asked permission to examine them.

" Be careful of the poisoned heads of the arrows," he said, unslinging his *ika* " (G) (quiver).

" Why do they have double heads ? " demanded Johnnie.

" The poison is in the bamboo barb (E), which fits over the

real head (D). The shaft (B) is called *shuri*, and the winged end *otzubu :* it is made of goose-feathers. The bow is made of untrimmed *ouruma*, and the cord is of the same plant as that used for making *ka*-strings."

" I see," said Johnnie. " You bind your bows with fine cord, but do not taper them as much as we do. What tree do you call *ouruma ?* "

The chief bade one of his people fetch a specimen ; and the man presently returned, bearing a branch which the Professor pronounced to be a species of yew.

" The quiver is of strips of wood bound with cherry-bark," said Fitz. " It combines strength and lightness."

The Professor pointed to the ornament, and said, —

" That is intended to represent water, and was invented by the Coreans."

" I think not," said Oto. " The design originally came from China. We obtained it from Corea, and the Ainos borrowed it from us. I do not think the Coreans were inventors of decorative forms."

SHUTTLE.

The chief then showed them the shuttle used by his wife in making bark cloth. It was of dark wood, very heavy, and ornamented with flowing patterns.

" Their weaving is very primitive," said Oto, " and is more like your mat-making than any thing else."

Just then the chief's wife came in, and, saluting them, said, — " All is ready."

Setta-eye rose, and led the way to a large hut, neatly covered with reeds, that stood about two hundred yards from his dwelling.

"That is yours," he said. "It is perfectly new, and was built expressly for your accommodation. I have appointed five servants to wait upon you. You can place your food and treasures in the storehouse behind."

"Oh, how delightful!" exclaimed Sallie, surveying the scene. "Just fancy: we are going to live in an Aino house, and to stay here a while."

"Why are those skulls put on the fence?" asked Fitz.

THE JEWETTS' HOME IN HOKUYAK-BETS

"That shows a famous hunter once lived near here," replied the chief. "We always put those trophies on stakes near his house, then the bad bears do not come and attack us. Do you see your servant? she is pounding millet for your attendant's supper."

They thanked him, after which he took his leave, saying, —

"You must go into your home unattended: it is yours."

The hut, contrary to Aino fashion, was divided into three

rooms, each of which was provided with a mat-covered bench. Habo said that Setta-eye had taken great pains to learn how foreign houses were made, and had sent runners to Hakodate to study architecture.

"This will be jolly," said Fitz. " But where are we going to cook? If we light a fire in here, we shall all be smothered."

Habo led the way to the back of the structure, where they found a shed under which some big stones were placed so as to form a rest for the iron pot (used by the Ainos), a curious article with four rings inside the lid. Mrs. Jewett said she could bake in it, and that they had cooked many a chowder at pic- nics on a similar arrangement of rocks. Before nightfall Oto, who was quite handy, had con- structed a temporary table, and

IRON POT.

the travellers sat down to what Fitz termed a square meal.

" I hope we shall stay here a year, sir," he said to his father. " Nothing like studying the habits of a people on the spot. To- morrow I am going to ask Chief Setta-eye to go bear-hunting."

" I think we ought to visit the chief, and thank him for his kindness," said the Professor. " Come, boys."

They found their friend entertaining five of the old men of his tribe, and dancing the crow-dance for their amusement.

It was very comical to see him move his hands, and hop first on one foot and then on the other; while a male servant solemnly marched round the party, and filled their cups from a lacquer vessel.

" You will please excuse us from remaining," said the Pro- fessor. " We all feel very tired. Good-night."

"*Saramba*" (good-by), cried the Ainos, making their graceful salutation, and stroking their shaggy beards.

The drinking was continued all night and the next day in honor of the foreigners, and, but for the exhaustion of the *saké*-tubs, would probably have been continued indefinitely.

Setta-eye did not call upon his visitors for nearly a week ; and when he came his eyes were red, as though he had not

SETTA-EYE ENTERTAINING HIS FRIENDS

recovered from his dissipation.   He informed the Professor that he was about to inflict the punishment of *oukari* upon a man who had been condemned for a serious crime ; adding, by way of explanation, —

" This ceremony differs greatly from *oukari*, the trial of strength.   The man who is to suffer deserves severe punishment, and is not permitted to determine when he has had enough : I decide that."

" When will the sentence be carried out ? " inquired the Professor.

"At noon," answered the chief. "I will conduct you to the place, and see that you have seats."

At the appointed time the gentlemen of the party accompanied their host to a level spot overlooking the Bear River, where they found quite a crowd of Ainos.

A mat was spread upon the ground, and three old men, appointed to act as witnesses, knelt upon it in a row; then a sad-looking woman was brought forward by her father, and placed upon Setta-eye's left, and her husband took up his position on the chief's right. By that time the foreign visitors had settled themselves upon a rude bench made of logs covered with mats, that their host had provided for them.

At a signal from Setta-eye, the prisoner was brought in between two of his friends, who, turning him with his back towards the spectators, removed his upper garment, and stripped him to the waist. He was a muscular, determined-featured savage, who could evidently take severe punishment. The chief gave another signal, whereupon the prisoner's wife advanced, carrying a covered tub filled with water, and a branch of dwarf bamboo. As she uncovered the vessel, a wiry-looking Aino, armed with a club bound with rawhide, emerged from among the spectators, and, taking up his place behind the prisoner, stood ready to administer the punishment.

Setta-eye commanded silence by waving his hand, then said, —

"This man has robbed his friend's wife, and must therefore be punished. Now hit him hard, and do not be afraid."

The club-swinger plied his weapon with a will, and the prisoner bore the pain with the greatest stoicism. At every fifth blow his wife advanced, and sprinkled his back with water.

It was some time before the fellow showed signs of weaken-
ing : however, finally he cried out that he was sorry, and would
never repeat the offence.   When the culprit was led away, Fitz
inquired the nature of the prisoner's crime; whereupon the
chief said, —

" It is against our custom for any one to enter another man's
house without the permission of its owner.   The prisoner had
been guilty of this offence, and had stolen the earrings belong-

PUNISHMENT OF OUKARI.

ing to the complainant's wife.   What punishment do you award
for such a crime ? "

" It all depends," said Fitz to Habo. " Tell him that a
criminal is sometimes sent to state's prison, but if he has
political influence he is allowed to continue his dishonorable
career."

" I do not understand you," she replied, with a puzzled air.
" When an Aino commits a crime, he receives suitable punishment."

Fitz smiled, and remarked to his father in English, —

" These Yezo-jin are real savages. They do not understand political influence."

" They will soon learn," replied the Professor. " It is not a study that requires a high degree of intelligence."

The chief, who had listened respectfully, said, —

" I am about to judge between two women who both lay claim to a *shitoki*. Each says that the jewel belongs to her, and I am going to decide the matter."

" How do you proceed ? " inquired Johnnie.

He invited them to follow him, and led the way to a spot where they saw a large iron kettle placed upon a mat, and two Aino women, who were regarding each other very angrily.

The vessel, which probably contained three gallons, was brim-full of boiling water. As soon as the Americans had seated themselves, the chief addressed the women as follows : —

" *Echokai tu ainu ne, khcmanuku ishka khetanea ?* " (" Which of you is the culprit ? ")

" I would like to have my *shitoki*," said the elder. " That girl has my property, and will not restore it to me."

" Produce it," said Setta-eye.

" Indeed it is mine," answered the younger. " It was given me when I was married. I lost it one day when I was out in the woods."

" How did you get it again ? " demanded the chief.

" I saw it in her hut, and took possession of it."

She then reluctantly drew the coveted article from her bosom, and handed it to the chief ; who, holding it at arm's-length, said, —

" This is a very simple affair. Only one of you can be the true owner : the other must tell a falsehood. It is easy to

determine which is in the right.   There are three stones in that
kettle of hot water: whichever of you removes them without
scalding her hands is innocent, and shall take the *shitoki*.   The
water will not injure the one who has an honest heart."

Fitz chuckled, and was about to comment upon the rude
ordeal; when his father checked him, and said, —

SAIMON.   ORDEAL BY HOT WATER.

"All primitive races practised the same punishment."

"We call this *saimon*," said Habo.   "It never fails to
detect the wrong-doer."

The claimants "shed tears like rain," and for a time neither
appeared desirous of scalding her fingers: however, after
awhile the younger one bared her arm, and, thrusting it into the
boiling water, fished out a stone, then cried to her opponent, —

"Now you do the same."

The old woman made a great show of contempt, and advanced toward the vessel as though about to answer her challenger; but paused, and said in a grumbling tone, —

"You can take the trumpery *shitoki*."

Having announced her determination, she darted a look of hatred at the successful candidate, and retired.

Setta-eye handed the jewel to its proper owner, who put it about her neck, and rejoined her friends.

"The *saimon* is a very old custom, and it works well, remarked the chief. "Rogues are deterred from committing crimes through fear of having to undergo this trial."

He conducted them home, and on parting said, —

"The hunters have just brought me word that they have trapped a fine bear in the mountains. Would you like to join me in killing it?"

"Very much indeed," said Fitz. "I have promised a number of skins to my friends, and wish to secure them as soon as possible."

Habo awoke them the next morning by calling,—

"The hunters are here. Will you please rise, or the bear may get out of the pit."

"We will fix him," said Fitz. "Where is my rifle, Johnnie, and my cartridge-belt?"

"Where you left them last night," was the quiet response.

Sallie, who heard the conversation, rose, made the party some coffee, and as she served it said. —

"I am sorry I cannot go with you. I wish I were a boy: you have all the fun. Cannot I accompany you at a distance?"

"Did you ever hear such foolishness!" cried Fitz. "The idea of your wanting to go bear-hunting, Sallie Jewett! You would scream if you saw a bear twelve miles off, unless he were in a cage. You stay at home, and have something toothsome for us on our return. A nice hunt we should have if we took you with us!"

The Professor fairly bristled with weapons; while his sons and Oto, in addition to their rifles, carried knives and a battery of small-arms.

AINO HUNTERS.

They found the hunters standing near a wood-pile at the back of the house, waiting to be summoned.

The Ainos, father and son, spite of their rough appearance, were gentle-mannered.

"Where are your weapons?" asked Fitz.

"Up in the mountain," answered the elder. "We only use spears and bows and arrows."

The men then spoke to one another in a low tone.

"They are afraid of being killed," said Habo. "Ainos are not used to your weapons."

"We won't hurt them," said Fitz, in a re-assuring tone. "Tell them we know how to use these as well as they do their bows."

The younger of the men tied deer-hide gaiters upon his legs; and, when Setta-eye joined the party, he led the way into the mountains.

The chief told them that bears were becoming very scarce, and where they formerly killed ten they with difficulty secured one.

"I see he has a stock of *inaho*" (god-sticks) "with him," said Fitz.

Oto nodded, and answered, —

"They never leave home without them. He won't have one in his quiver when he returns."

Ascending the mountain proved to be very hard work, and necessitated frequent stoppages in order to give the foreigners rest.

About ten o'clock they arrived at a gorge, at the far end of which was a cave containing the game, which proved to be a fine adult brown bear. Some branches of a tree had been fastened across the entrance, and the animal appeared to be securely caged.

It gnawed at the obstruction, and growled savagely, as though it would like to attack its captors.

"May I try my hand, sir?" said Fitz, unslinging his rifle.

"Not on any account," severely answered the Professor. "No sportsman would think of shooting an animal confined in that manner."

"I did not know," muttered the boy. "I thought it had to be killed. If it gets out, it will make things lively for us. It is as mad as a hornet that has lost its nest."

When Setta-eye found the foreigners would not kill the imprisoned animal, he took up his position about fifty yards from the cave, and shouted, —

"Now you are going to become a god."

He then thrust an *inaho* into the ground, motioned his dogs to keep quiet, and selecting an arrow shot it at the imprisoned animal, which, maddened with pain, beat against the obstruction to its liberty, and uttered the most piteous cries.

The Ainos discharged a shower of arrows, and finally rendered the poor brute so furious that it threw itself against the barrier, and broke it down.

"Leave it to me: I'll shoot it, I'll shoot it!" cried Fitz, advancing toward the creature.

SHOOTING A TRAPPED BEAR.

"Run, run, run!" shouted the Professor, Johnnie, and Oto, who dared not shoot for fear of hurting him.

"Run away!" shouted Setta-eye.

Fitz took no heed of their warnings, but levelled his piece at the animal, which was standing on the ruins of the barrier, swinging its head, and uttering sharp, savage growls.

The boy fired, striking the bear on the nose.

At four o'clock they bade farewell to their friends, and started. Oto and the Americans carried alpenstocks; but the Ainos, who all had heavy packs lashed to their shoulders, did not condescend to avail themselves of any such assistance.

The mist settled in the valleys, and hung in curd-like strata round the hill-tops, rendering the scene very weird. Before

SUNRISE.

long, the travellers' garments were saturated, and felt twice their usual weight.

"I wish some one would wring me out," laughingly remarked Johnnie.

"It is not so bad as riding among dank herbage," said Sallie. "Do you know, I rather enjoy this *excelsior* business."

They climbed on and on, until they reached a plateau overlooking a little lake, where they halted in order to see the sunrise.

Presently Habo pointed downward, and exclaimed, —

" There she is ! see how beautiful she looks ! "

The sight was certainly lovely ; for, reflected on the mirror-like surface, they beheld the crimson orb slowly emerge from its concealment, and illuminate the water with its brilliant rays. On turning, they saw the same sight above the mountain-tops.

" Oh, oh, oh ! " ejaculated Sallie. " Crimson and gold, violet and silver, purple and gray, in one glorious harmony ; this is " —

" Too, too utter ! " said Fitz, who was shivering. " If I miss having chills and fever, I don't know any thing about symptoms."

" Oh, come along ! " urged Johnnie. " We will not wake you so early another morning, brother dear."

As the sun rose, the mist vanished, and the travellers' clothes dried ; whereupon the boy recovered his spirits, and began to pick flowers.

" You, mother, shall have the white ones, and Sallie these dark-brown lilies trimmed with yellow," he said. " This reminds me of home."

He made two bouquets, and politely presented them to his parent and sister. Upon smelling their gifts, Mrs. Jewett made a gesture of disappointment, and Sallie exclaimed, —

" I love these blossoms of the wilderness ; " then, noticing her mother hastily discard hers, she added, " Why, mamma, what is the matter ? "

" These flowers were as white and pure-looking as wax, but their odor was unbearable," answered the lady. " As usual, one must not go by appearances."

" That is so," murmured thoughtful Johnnie. " There is many a black heart under a white skin, and *vice versa.*"

YEZO WILD FLOWERS.

Habo, who had listened to the conversation, inquired what was the matter, and, when she learned, said, —

"That *haa* plant is peculiar : its roots are good to eat, but it does not smell very nice. When we touch it, we always pinch our nostrils. They say the bad gods made it to deceive the Aino. We call the white flower *niyo-kai*" (wheel lily).

"The *haa* deceived me," said Fitz. "I think I must have got a chill, and lost my sense of smell."

"You are all right," said his mother.

As they halted for breakfast, they noticed an Aino seated in a valley, as though on the look-out for something.

"He is watching for bears," said Habo. "I know him very well; he is a most dutiful boy."

"At what time do your youths become of age?" inquired Johnnie.

At first she seemed puzzled : then she smiled, and said, —

"When they are married : until that time they live at home, and belong to their parents. Do you notice how very ragged his clothes are?"

"Yes," said Fitz : "his coat looks as though it had been used for a target. I wonder he does not get his mother to mend it for him."

"He is too dutiful to trouble her," replied Habo. "He has made several applications to the authorities for permission to marry, but has been refused."

"Why?" sympathetically inquired Sallie.

"Because he is not successful at hunting, or in raising crops," answered Habo. "When an Aino fails to pay his taxes, the government officials will not give him permission to marry."

"That is only just," said Mrs. Jewett. "If a man is unable to keep himself, he should not be allowed to take a wife."

" Poor fellow ! perhaps he is in love," said Sallie.

" Oh ! stuff and nonsense," said Fitz.   " Do you think that great looney sitting there, and holding on to a pole like a gorilla, was ever in love ?   I consider the Japanese authorities were perfectly right : he will not shoot a bear until he is gray-headed.   I believe his mother has spoilt him."

A LAZY AINO.

By the time the sun has attained its meridian, the travellers became very tired, and were glad enough to meet a young Japanese merchant, who told them they would find an Aino's hut in the woods about a quarter of a mile on their right.

" They own a spring of delicious water," he said, " and are very hospitable to strangers.   If you desire it, I will show you the way."   The Professor asked Habo if she knew the man, upon which she said, —

" Yes; but I do not like to visit him, because he would not take the blows at an *oukari* given by my father."

" You must put aside your social prejudices," said the Professor. " Come, we are very thirsty."

He did not know, that, according to Aino etiquette, the woman was supposed not to speak to such a cowardly person : however, Habo was too gentle to offer any further remonstrance.

They followed the merchant, and after a short walk arrived at the hut.

The Aino made his peculiar salutation, and invited them indoors ; his wife hurrying off with a lacquer vessel, with which she presently returned, saying, —

" I wish this cold water were *saké*."

" It tastes like lemonade," said Fitz. " How nice ! "

" They put a quantity of bruised sorrel in the spring," said the merchant. " This fellow possesses some very fine pieces of lacquer. Would you like to see them ? "

Three old Ainos came in, and, squatting, saluted the visitors ; then their host climbed a notched post, and reached dov.n some clean mats, which were spread upon the floor for the accommodation of the guests.

" Now show your treasures," said Habo.

The man saluted her, and, re-ascending the log, handed down several old swords, the scabbards of which were inlaid with mother-of-pearl, and beautifully lacquered.

" These belonged to his five-times-grandfather," said Habo. " They were given to his ancestor by a noble whose life he saved. One day the lord was travelling in great haste to reach Matsumai, but upon arriving here found the river so high that he would be delayed several weeks. This greatly troubled him, and he shed tears; on noticing which, that man's five-times-grandfather inquired the cause.

" ' Alas!" said the noble, 'I am indeed a miserable person.

JAPANESE CURIOS IN AINO HUT.

My aged mother in Matsumai is at the point of death, and desires very much to see me. Rather than imbitter her last moments, I prefer to jump into the river, and to end my miser-

able life, thus accompanying my parent along the lonely road.'
Then this man's five-times-grandfather spoke, saying, —

"'Up in the side of the valley, the walls of rock almost
touch one another; and in that spot grows a willow-tree.
Rather than that your mother shall suffer, we will risk our lives
to enable you to reach her. Please follow me.'

"Then he selected six companions; and, after taking a bundle of *inaho*, they started out, and ascended the mountain side.

"Upon arriving at the place, they saw the tall willow which,
about three feet from the rock, forked into two huge limbs.
This man's five-times-grandfather climbed the strongest branch,
and two companions followed him, each carrying an *inaho*"
(god-stick) "in his hand. Their weight gradually bent the
willow until the limb bowed across the chasm, and they were
enabled to seize the grass and rocks on the other side. Then
they lifted large pieces of stone, and placed them so as to
secure it, and, handing the noble an *inaho*, bade him cross the
bridge they had made.

"'I am in great fear,' he said, 'never having been trained
to perform acrobatic feats : still, remembering that my aged
mother is desirous of seeing me, I will not care for the risk,
even though it lead to my death;' saying which, he stepped
upon the branch, and, though his heart sank very low in his
body, he crossed in safety.

"He gave this man's relative many beautiful things, among
them being these swords."

"Will he sell them?" inquired Professor Jewett, who was
an enthusiastic collector of Japanese weapons.

Habo shook her head, and said, —

"He would never part with those swords. They were given
to him on his marriage, and will belong to his children."

It uttered a sound between a snarl and a bark, lowered its head, and made swiftly for the lad ; who, nothing daunted, calmly reloaded his weapon, and shot the monster a second time.

"Run, run!" cried the agonized Professor, tugging at the trigger of his rifle.

Fitz coolly reloaded, and, when the bear was within three yards of him, pulled for the third time. To his horror he found that the hammer would not work, and in another instant he felt the breath of the animal upon his face.

CHAPTER VII.

BEAR-HUNTING.

He who plays with fire should not complain about his burns. — OLD PROVERB.
He who undertakes to catch a bear must not cry over his wounds. — AINO
SAYING.

FITZ did not know any thing about his rescue, a blow from the bear's paw having rendered him insensible.

Upon seeing his son fall, the Professor clubbed his rifle, and dealt the animal a tremendous blow between the eyes. Johnnie and Oto rushed in, pressed the muzzles of their weapons against the animal's chest, and fired; then the Ainos uttered frightful cries, and attacked the bear with their spears.

The poor brute fought desperately hard, and before it died wounded several of the savages, who, regardless of its hugging, approached very closely, and as they thrust their spears taunted it, saying, —

" You think you are a god, but we can overcome you."

While they were despatching the creature, the Professor, Oto, and Johnnie were attending to Fitz. They carried him toward a spring of water, and bathed his face until he regained consciousness; as he did so, the Ainos gave a shout of victory.

The boy opened his eyes, and, glancing up at his father, said, —

" I guess that b'ar hunted me. It is fortunate Sallie did not accompany us at a distance."

"Are you hurt anywhere?" inquired the young doctor.

"I don't know," answered Fitz. "I feel kinder dizzy. I believe there is something the matter with my neck."

When his coat was removed, Oto discovered that the bear had clawed the sufferer's shoulder, and lacerated the muscles of his back.

"Oh! it is only a scratch or two," said Fitz. "One must expect such things when they tackle a bear. Just smooth the rough places down, and put on one of your honorable plasters. I shall be all right in a few minutes."

He rose, but was seized with giddiness; and it was some time before he felt well enough to continue the conversation.

Setta-eye and the other Ainos, who were very much concerned, watched him with the greatest anxiety.

Presently the chief went to the bear, which by that time had been denuded of its skin, and was suspended from the limb of a tree, as a farmer hangs a dressed hog. He took an *inaho*, and thrust it into the liver; then cutting off a portion of the latter offered it to Fitz, saying, —

"Eat this quickly: it will make you very strong."

This was too much for the boy, who, in spite of his weakness, was as full of fun as ever.

"Make me strong, eh?" he murmured. "It is Aino tonic, I suppose. Much obliged. I made a vow to Bindzuri, not to take any medicine for ten years. Kindly eat it for me: it will do me just as much good."

"There is nothing serious the matter with you," said the young doctor. "Do you think you are sufficiently recovered to walk home? If you are not, we will improvise an ambulance for you."

"Not if I can prevent you," was the quiet rejoinder.

" What would mother and Sallie think if they saw a procession of that sort descending the mountain? No, thank you, Dr. Nambo."

" I will go ahead and tell them," said the Professor. " You can rest, and need not hurry home."

When his father had departed, Fitz remarked, —

" This must be a cool country in the winter."

" It is," answered Oto. " The thermometer goes down until you cannot see the mercury, and the wind blows hard enough to take you off your feet. Some years ago my grandfather, who was very fond of hunting, came up here to shoot bears."

" Did they chase him?"

" Oh, no!" answered Oto. " He engaged the Ainos to dig a pit, which he baited with sweet-potatoes. The natives built a temporary shelter near the spot, and put *inaho* outside for luck. One morning they came to him in a great hurry, saying that the bear was in the pit, and would my grandfather hasten to kill the creature? My relative started at a great pace, being very anxious to secure the prize. Upon reaching the hut, the Ainos entered in order to warm their frozen fingers; but my ancestor kept right on, making great leaps over the snow, and causing the scabbards of his swords to rattle noisily. This greatly alarmed the bear, which in its struggles presently scrambled to the top of the pit. Noticing this, my grandfather halted, and discharged his weapon. The bear, infuriated by the wound, contrived to escape, and made its way up the mountain side; seeing which, my grandfather pressed on, and forgetting the pitfall tumbled in. The Ainos, not having witnessed his accident, continued to warm themselves, while he struggled to do as the animal had done. In vain he shouted: his voice was muffled as though he were in a well, and the watchers failed to

OTO'S GRANDFATHER HUNTING.

hear him. At nightfall they came out with torches, and discovered his whereabouts, he having been in the hole eight
hours. I have a picture of this incident, and will give it to you
to show your friends."

"Come," said Fitz. "Let us be moving. I am afraid
mother will worry on my account."

As they descended the mountain they heard shouts behind
them, and, looking back, beheld an enormous bear stealing
away from the huntsmen ; who, as they ran, rapidly discharged
their arrows.

"Let us have a shot at it," said Fitz. "Give me my rifle,
Johnnie."

"You have had enough sport for to-day," answered his
brother.

While they were speaking, the animal was sneaking down
the ravine, and Oto was "drawing a bead on it."

The report was sharp ; and the ball struck its object, causing
the bear to quicken its pace.

Fitz took his rifle from his brother, and, spite of his lame
back, raised it to his shoulder, and pulled. The missive took
effect just behind the bear's shoulder, and rolled the animal
over.

"'Rah! 'Rah!" shouted the excited lad. "One for our
side. Ain't I glad I came! I'll get a fine skin, and bear's-
grease enough to last sister all her life."

They approached the carcass, and, after examining it, told
the Ainos to be very careful in removing the pelt ; then made
the best of their way home.

Mrs. Jewett and Sallie were on the lookout for them ; and,
when they saw the party, ran forward exclaiming, —

"Fitz, why did you rush into such danger? Are you badly
hurt?"

FITZ'S BEAR.

" I have killed a bear anyhow," he replied.

" You mean that it nearly killed you," said Sallie.   " O Fitz Jewett! you have given us such a scare! "

" You are not as badly scared as the bear, sis," he slyly answered.   " He is what the Ainos call a *shigoma.* — Mother, you shall have the skin for a rug."

At first Mrs. Jewett thought he was joking: however, when Oto and Johnnie confirmed his statement, she said, —

" I am both glad and sorry, — glad because you have been so fortunate ; and sorry because I know, now you have secured one skin, you will not rest until you have a dozen."

When the Professor heard the news, he said, —

" I congratulate you, my son.   Now take a rest."

Habo was much concerned when she discovered that Fitz had been injured.   She insisted upon seeing the scratches, and wanted to apply an Aino remedy to them; remarking, —

" You encountered the chief of the bears.   The creature was once a great tree in the mountains: now its life is cut off, it will again become a tree.   It was a wonder you escaped so easily.   You ought to take a sweat to get rid of the poison."

" I would rather take a cup of coffee," said the merry fellow.   " As for rubbing in your ointment, you must ask Dr. Nambo."

Oto decided that it was unnecessary, and said a good bath would be of greater service than any Aino specific.

" We have secured a *saké*-tub," said the Professor.   " You will find it already filled in your room."

That evening the travellers enjoyed a meal of bear-meat, at the conclusion of which they inspected the skins brought down from the mountain by the Aino.

Setta-eye promised to have them dressed, and forwarded to

Hakodate by the time they returned from Saghalin : then saluting them in his graceful fashion was retiring, when he paused,
and, addressing the Professor, said, —

"We are going to hold the festival of *Iyomante*" (killing
and worshipping the bear). "It is usually done in the fall ; but
last year, at the appointed time, the *shigoma* was very sick.
Now he is quite well again, and we are all anxious to make a
god of him. I have decided to do this to-morrow. Can you
be present ? "

"Yes, indeed," was the reply: "both myself and friends
would like to witness the rites."

When he was gone, Habo introduced a middle-aged woman,
named Ochin, who said that she had been the foster-mother of
the bear that was to be sacrificed.

" Foster-mother ? " said Fitz. "What does she mean ? "

" Well, you see the bear is taken from its mother when it is
a few days old," said Habo. "It is a little, blind, helpless
creature, and requires nursing like a baby. If the foster-
mother is good-tempered, the bear will be amiable. If she is
bad, the animal will be savage. We are very careful in appoint-
ing the bear's attendant."

" What have you in that bag around your neck ? " inquired
Mrs. Jewett.

The woman untied the receptacle, and, taking a paper from
it, replied, —

" This is my marriage-permit. It was given me by the
Japanese officials, and a similar one was handed to my husband."

" Why is there only half a seal on it ? " inquired Sallie.

" Both certificates were written on one piece of paper, and
the seal was placed between them," explained the woman.

"This proves I am the wife of Toki, the person who owns the other half."

"What is the Aino name for married woman?" asked Fitz.

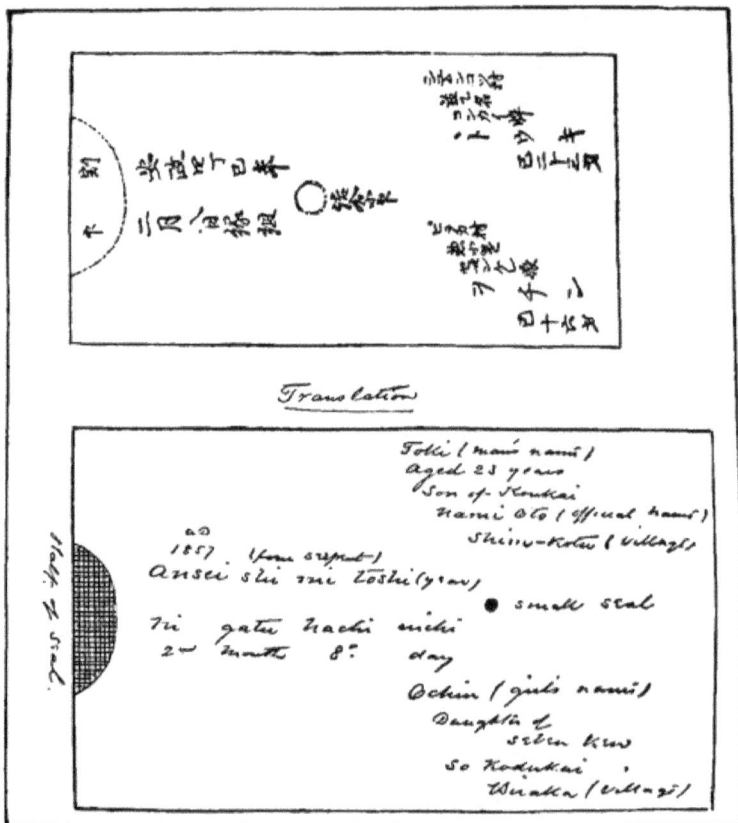

AINO MARRIAGE-PERMIT.

"*Machi*," answered Habo. "An unmarried female is termed *menoco*, and a young girl *mencoshi*. As soon as we are married, we cut our hair across the forehead."

"What we call bang it," said Fitz. "Our ladies, of all

ages, have their hair banged. Why do some of yours let it grow long, and hang over their eyes?"

"That is a sign of mourning," said Habo. "When we lose out relations, we let our hair grow for three years: it makes us look very sad. The other day you asked me why we tattooed our hands, and why no Aino likes you to look into the window of his house. I have inquired of the chief's mother, who is a very aged person, and knows every thing. She says, in ancient times there lived a god named Kocha. He was six feet high, and had long, powerful hands. His houses, which were made of earth, were all over the land. Every one admired his skill in fishing and hunting; and he was very generous, — often putting bear-meat and fish in at the windows of the Ainos' huts, though he never taught the people to capture either the seal or the bear. At last he became offended at our ancestors' ignorance, and took his wife, and quitted the land. Since that time no Aino likes any one to look through the window of his house, believing that such an act should only be done by the gods. But when an Aino is going to fish for seals, or hunt a bear, his harpoon or his spear and bows and arrows are passed through the window; and on his return every thing he captures is taken into the house through the same aperture. The god-stick, placed near a dead bird on the window-sill, represents the god Kocha."

"But how about the tattooing?" inquired Sallie.

"Kocha-kami's wife, who was a very beautiful woman, had her mouth, arms, and hands tattooed," answered Habo. "The traces of the god and his wife are seen in many places; and we sometimes find pieces of pottery, and the jewels they wore, when we dig new land to plant millet. Aino women, wishing to preserve the memory of Kocha-kami's wife, and to possess

her virtues, tattoo themselves as she did. Now will you please
excuse me, as the chief has sent us some *saké*, and I have to
serve it to the men."

She saluted them, and retired; and they presently saw her

filling large cups with the wine
from some lacquer vessels placed
on a mat in the cook-house.

"I wonder the Japanese don't
prevent the Ainos from drinking so much," said Johnnie.

Oto smiled, and answered, —

"Our government does try,
but it can no more prevent
drunkenness among the Ainos

HABO SERVING SAKÉ.

than yours can among the Indians. We no longer give them
yearly allowances of *saké*."

"Come, boys," said the Professor. "I think you had
better retire. To-morrow we will have to rise early to witness
the *Iyomante*."

CHAPTER VIII.

IYOMANTE.

" To-day we worship you as a god:
Therefore eat what we offer, and enjoy yourself."
AINO'S SPEECH TO THE BEAR.

FIVE o'clock, and time to rise," said the Professor. "Habo tells us that to-day's entertainment is called *Hinzinzo*" (feeding the bear). "The men of the tribe have been up since dawn, making *inaho*. As soon as the sun is over the mountain, the ceremony will begin: so rise, my boys, and get your breakfast."

Fitz yawned, and said in a grumbling tone, —

"I wonder folks go to bed at all in this country. They could feed the bear just as well at noon as at sunrise. It has to be killed anyhow."

"You are very much like a bear, brother," said Sallie from the next room.

"How?" he inquired.

"You are always growling," she replied. "Just think of it: we shall witness a ceremony that has seldom been seen by foreigners, and learn how they conduct the rite of bear-worship."

"I wish I could find my boots," mumbled her brother. "I have not had a wink of sleep all night."

"Why, Fitz dear! we heard you snoring," said Mrs. Jewett.

"Yes, mother, if I am very tired, I snore when I am wide

awake," he quickly answered.   " Did not sleep a wink, mother,
all night — fact."

After he had dressed, Oto came in, and, rubbing his hands,
exclaimed, —

" We are going to see some fun to-day.   The Ainos are out
in full force ; and Setta-eye is wearing his crown, and looks as
imposing as a drum-major."

MAKING INAHO.

Breakfast was quickly despatched ; after which the chief
called upon them, and, saluting them gravely, said, —

" Every thing is ready."

They followed him to a spot near his hut, where they found
the bear's cage, surrounded by Ainos, who were   dancing,
shouting, or whittling *inaho.*

"Why, there are thousands of the god-sticks made," remarked Johnnie.   "What are they going to do with them?"

Habo explained, —

" Those will be used during the next three days."

They watched the men, and noticed the dexterous manner in which they turned out the *inaho*.

After the visitors had been accommodated with seats, Setta-eye gave the signal for the dance to begin; whereupon the women brought the bear some dried fish, and, addressing it, said, —

" Honor us by eating this poor food."

The foster-mother next advanced, and, speaking to the animal, said, —

" I beg of you to be very patient, and not to bite, my son."

The bear growled, and taking the fish proceeded to munch it with great relish. While he was enjoying himself, three Aino women and ten men approached the cage, and began to stamp, whine, and dance, as they did so, shouting, —

> "To-day we worship you as a god,
> Therefore eat what we offer, and enjoy yourself."

All of the tribe took turns in thus dancing and singing; the entertainment continuing until sunset, when a miniature fence was made round his cage with *inaho*, and he was left alone for the night.

At sunrise the woman who had attended him spread a new mat of red and brown reeds in front of the cage, then withdrew the lower bars, and, bowing, said, —

" Honorable god, please come out."

The creature obeyed, and, rising upon its haunches, rubbed its nose, and made a peculiar whimpering noise, which affected the woman to tears.

In a few moments the Americans heard a great shouting; and presently Setta-eye appeared, grasped the bear by its ears, and rode on its back.

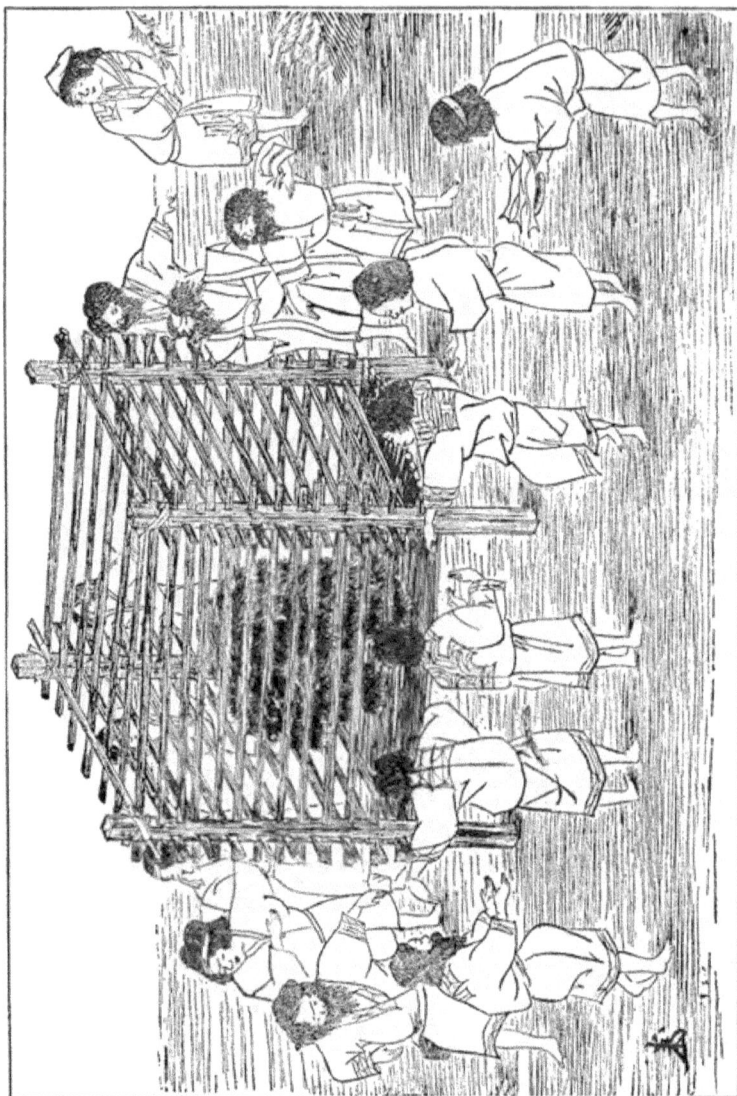

H NZINZO DANCE.

The animal shambled round, uttered loud growls, and charged right and left at the people.

This amusement was kept up until noon, when the chief gave a signal, and every one rushed for their bows and blunt arrows. Even the little children, provided with these weapons, were brought in the mothers' arms, or Indian fashion, on their backs, to fire a shot.

Ropes were secured to the bear's hind-legs, and he was pulled hither and thither until he became really dangerous.

As the sun descended, Setta-eye turned towards the western mountain, and said, —

" Bear, I make you happy."

At this signal, his son advanced to the victim, and discharged a blunt arrow at him. A shower of the missives followed, and caused the poor brute to rear, snarl, and snap at every thing within his reach.

AINO BABIES.

In a little while he was led back to his cage, and secured for the night.

The ceremony of the next day was a very simple one. At sunrise the bear was let out of his cage, and conducted to a place where two large timbers were laid upon the ground. When he was fairly on these, a beam was lifted upon his neck, and, in the twinkling of an eye, loaded down with Ainos. As the executioners squeezed the life out of the poor thing, they chanted in a mournful way, in order to drown its cries and the lamentations of its foster-mother, who, seated near the bear's head, wept and rocked herself with grief, while her child exclaimed, —

"*Pirika, pirika!*" (good, good.)

" See-saw, Margery Daw," said Fitz, as the Ainos moved up and down like schoolboys on a plank.

TORMENTING THE BEAR.

" Please do not interrupt the ceremony," whispered Sallie.

" Circus, you mean," he retorted. " Poor old bear! he won't have a kick in him when they get through."

The foster-mother's husband next advanced with a sword, with which he touched the bear's eyes, nose, and ears, all the male Ainos following his example; after which millet-seed was thrown among the crowd.

"That is to make them strong when hunting," whispered Habo.

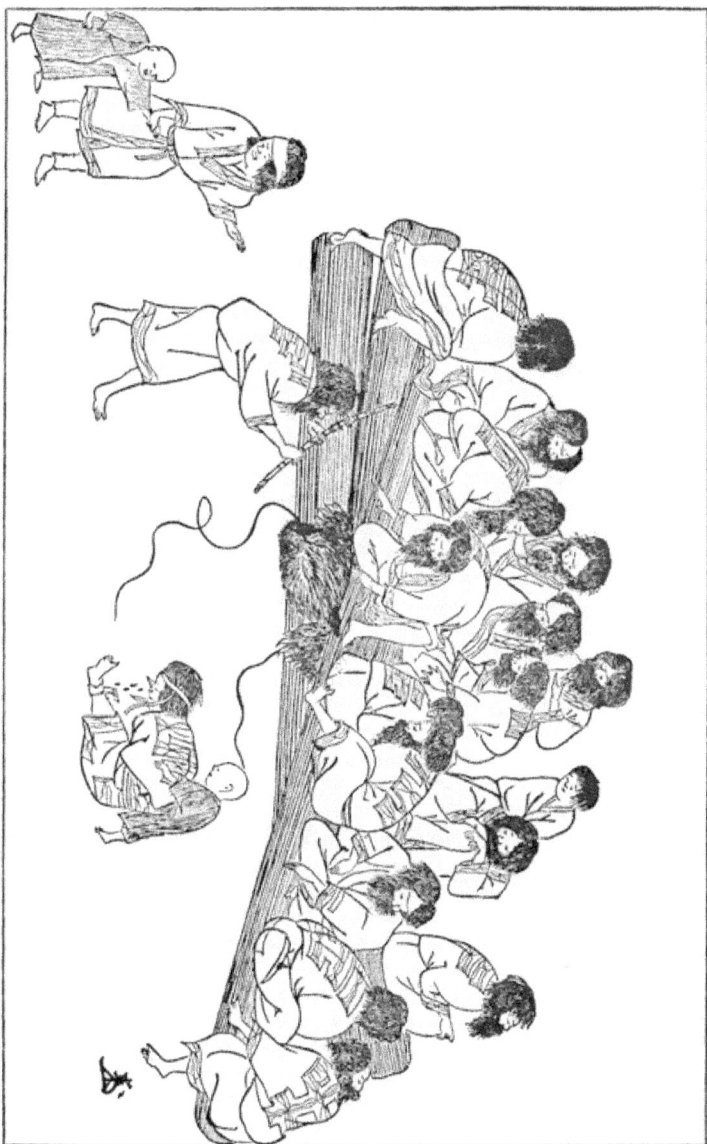

DEATH OF THE BEAR.

"Come," said Mrs. Jewett, "I have seen enough of this. Let us go home. I am tired out."

"What a primitive race they are!" remarked the Professor.

"Quite so," said his wife, — "almost too primitive for me. I think their see-sawing the bear to death was most barbarous."

"Mr. Bergh ought to be here," said Sallie, who agreed with her mother.

"The Aino would not care if he were," said Johnnie. "They would just yell, and go ahead; and Mr. Bergh would have to do as we did, leave them alone. These children of nature do not know they are acting cruelly."

On the following day the chief called upon his visitors, and, after saluting them gravely, said, —

"Now every thing is ready, will you come and see us worship the *shigame*?"

As the party passed through the village, they noticed all the Ainos were busily engaged making *inaho*, which were placed in front of the huts, in the window-apertures, and on all prominent places. Every one was dressed in his best robes; the women wore their jewelry, and the men their swords; even the yellow, wolf-like dogs, of which there were hundreds, having a sleek look as though they had been brushed for the occasion.

"This is evidently a very solemn ceremonial," remarked the Professor. "Fitz, I trust you will be discreet, and not make remarks that will cause these poor people to feel mortified."

"They do not understand what I say, sir," answered the boy. "Besides, I would not hurt their feelings on any account: they might stop the obsequies."

His father frowned, and was about to reply, when they arrived at a cleared place in the rear of the village, where they beheld a matted enclosure, the back of which was surmounted with peeled branches of trees decorated with the skulls of bears, many *inaho*, and weapons.

The Americans were conducted to rude seats, covered with skins placed on new mats of red and brown reeds.

" We shall have an excellent view here," said Sallie. " Oh ! isn't this interesting? There is the poor bear lying on the mat."

" That is only his skin," said Fitz, who had regarded it critically. " Oto says they finished the body at supper last night. They are very sensible heathen : they don't mind making soup of their gods."

" Hush !" said the Professor. " What are these old men going to do?"

" Wish they would give us a programme," murmured Fitz.

Habo, who knelt near them, bowed and whispered, —

" These are three chiefs of other tribes, who have come to witness the festival of Iyomante. Setta-eye's wife is putting a mat on the ground where they are to sit, to show that this tribe wishes to pay them great respect."

The patriarchs took their places, the senior on the right and the junior on the left. All of them had shaggy heads of hair, heavy eyebrows and moustache, and trimmed beards, and were otherwise as hairy as bears, which they strongly resembled.

" What enormous earrings they wear !" said Johnnie to his sister. " It is strange, the men of all semi-barbarous nations should use those adornments."

While the chiefs were seating themselves, the whole village had assembled, and taken their places on either side of the foreign guests.

Setta-eye, who was very dignified, waited until every thing

was quiet: then gracefully saluting the Americans, introduced the old men as follows:—

"These elders are from tribes through whose districts you will pass on your way northward. They desire to salute you, and to say their lives are at your disposal. The first is named Poro-Parumbe, the second Kuré Kina, the third Taiki Kamoi-yashi" (ghost of a flea).

"I wish we only encountered the latter," said Johnnie. "That old fellow was misnamed."

His father made a gesture of caution; and the three chiefs

AINO CHIEFS SALUTING STRANGERS.

placed their left hands over their right, and began to rub them. This they continued to do for over five minutes; during which time they looked very grave, and regarded the foreigners with great reverence.

At a signal from Setta-eye, they raised their hands, and placed them on the top of their heads.

"That," whispered Habo, "means, they respect you so much, that they wish to place you on their heads."

"Sit on them?" inquired Fitz. "Not to-day, thank you."

Setta-eye made another signal, seeing which the three chiefs brought their hands down over their faces and beards, and uttered a whining noise, ending with a sharp cry like the bark of a dog. When this had been repeated three times, they rose, and joined the spectators.

Setta-eye bowed, and, pointing to the enclosure, said (his speech being translated by Habo), —

"To-day we have built that god-fence, in order to honor the deity who lies there. You see it is formed of nice new mats, and that we have adorned it with the skulls of the god-bears who have gone before this one, with Kocha-kami" (ancient-god) "*inaho*, with old swords, bows and arrows, leather aprons, and *oukari*-clubs. The *arukitsufu*" (god-bear) "reclines with dignity upon a new mat, with his nose sniffing at cups of wine and oil. On either side of him are beautiful articles given our ancestors by the gods" (Japanese officials), "and the entrance is adorned with wooden vases containing bamboo-grass. The god has rings in his ears, and a sword on his left side ; and those boxes contain the clothes he is going to wear, now he is a deity."

Setta-eye then bowed and retired. Immediately after this, three mats were placed in front of the enclosure, and the chief, having put on a *kami-shimo* (ceremonial coat, that has wing-like projections on the shoulders), removed his crown, and knelt directly opposite the bear, his eldest son being on his right, and his youngest on his left. The three old chiefs then took up their positions on the mat upon his left, the master of the ceremonies on the mat upon his right, while the foster-mother of the bear, with her husband and child, were honored with places behind him.[1]

"How exceedingly interesting !" murmured the Professor.

The chief bowed his head to the mat, uttered the peculiar

[1] *Vide* Frontispiece.

Aino cry, terminating in a sharp bark, after which, taking a cup that had been filled by his son, dipped a *saké*-stick in it, and made three libations to the bear. This done, he solemnly raised his moustache with the stick, and drank the wine. He performed the ceremony thrice, the privileged ones on the mats repeating the action once.

The servants, from time to time, brought fresh supplies of *saké*, fish, and rice; and the ceremony soon resembled a picnic, much food being consumed and *saké* drank in honor of the god.

Two ancient swords were then brought by an old man, and laid before the bear; after which Setta-eye offered it more wine and food, and said in a very impressive manner, —

" *Churu kamoi tanewa kokuno kamoi in akatsu, tan nakinetemate siniriuiso wan. Shekan na kamoi nia mutsu Oya wa churu ki nankoru kuno shu tachikanatene ye chiroku kanan kanan hatsu chiman meshina.*"

SERVING WINE AT IYOMANTE.

("My god, to-day I, the chief, send you forth as a god. If you come again — as a little bear — next year, I will take care of you. Now you kindly leave.")

"How intensely interesting!" said the Professor. "Our ancestors must have practised just such rites. This is looking back thousands of years."

"They require enlightenment," quietly replied his wife. "To me this scene is very saddening."

"I am afraid they would not value our teaching," said Johnnie. "You see the *Iyomante* combines a feed of bear-soup with much *saké*-drinking : they would not care to exchange such a faith for ours."

"Jes' so," said Fitz, whose eyes twinkled with merriment. "Besides, they could not make soup of their teachers."

"That will do, my son," gently remarked his mother.

OURI SALUTATION.

The rest of the ceremony consisted in drinking *saké*, which did not prove very interesting to the foreigners, who, after thanking Setta-eye, returned home.

As they neared their house, they saw two Ainos, a man and woman, squatting on the ground, holding each other's hands, and making a dismal howling noise.

"What are they doing?" asked Mrs. Jewett.

" Performing *ouri*" (salutation), said Habo. "They are brother and sister who have been parted: watch them."

The man held the woman's hand for a few seconds, then, suddenly releasing his hold, grasped her by both ears, and uttered the Aino cry. Then they stroked one another down the face and shoulders, and, once more clasping hands, shed tears of joy.

"These people are very glad to see one another," said Habo. "That man has been on the coast fishing, and has only just returned."

" I thought they were sick," said Fitz. "Why do you always bark like that?"

" We do it to honor our ancestors," she replied. "It is an old Aino fashion."

Presently they encountered one of their servants, who, as they passed her, knelt, and placed her right forefinger on her upper lip.

"What is Matek-isep signalling about?" inquired Johnnie.

" She is very polite," answered Habo. "When an Aino girl meets a friend, she salutes in that way."

" I suppose that is another old Aino custom," said Fitz.

" Yes: it was taught our ancestors by the wife of the god Kocha. An Aino girl is too bashful to speak."

Upon entering the house they saw a large iron pot containing a stew made of bear's-flesh, ground millet, *haa*-roots, and fish-oil.

" This is your share of the feast," said Habo. "The chief has sent it with his respects. It is very good, and such food will make your hair beautiful and glossy."

" It would turn mine gray," murmured Fitz. "I · have heard that bear's grease is a good thing for the hair, but I decline to take it internally. This is the worst chowder I ever saw."

As he spoke in English, Habo had not understood him:

AINO WOMAN'S RECOGNITION.

however, she guessed by his tone that he was not anxious to partake of the meal, so she said in an aside, —

" The servants will be very happy to eat that for you. It is very strengthening, and makes one live a long time."

"Go ahead, then," he whispered. "May you all live to be a hundred years old! I do not envy you."

"Come to the door, and look at these men," said Sallie. "Here is a curious sight."

They joined her, and beheld two Ainos kneeling close to each other, knee to knee, and uttering the dog-like cry.

"What is that caper?" said Fitz to Habo.

"That is *ouri* too," she replied. "Those men are relatives. The old one has grasped his son's ears, and now they are going to cry."

The men did as she said, and continued to weep for over twenty minutes; after which they calmly rose, lighted their pipes, and went on their way.

"We shed tears when we meet after long separation," said Habo.

"We do it when we are parting from our friends," said Sallie. "We very seldom cry when we meet them."

MEETING OF FATHER AND SON

"You used to cry when aunt Allen visited us," mischievously remarked Fitz.

"Don't tease me so, brother," she replied. "I do not believe you like her any more than I do."

"Who is your aunt Allen?" asked Oto. "I fail to remember ever having seen her."

" No," said Johnnie. " She never inflicted herself upon our household after you came to stay with us."

" I suppose she did not want to associate with a Japanese," said Oto, smiling; " or, maybe, she took me for a heathen Chinee."

" I will tell you," said Sallie. " Aunt Allen is not at all nice : she is mean, suspicious, narrow-minded, and insincere. But that is her misfortune. She has been, all her life, in a village, and has never known the great world. She hates the English, because our ancestors had a little unpleasantness with them ; will not speak to her neighbor, on account of the latter not belonging to her church ; and is, altogether, an unlovable being. But papa says we ought to overlook her faults, because she has never had an opportunity of seeing any place but West Stonehill : so we try to endure her society."

" We have such people in Japan," said the young doctor ; " and to them applies the proverb, ' The toad in the well knows not the great ocean.' "

They dined upon some delicious venison and salmon, sent them by Setta-eye, who, during their stay in his village, had supplied their table with fish and game.

Hokuyak-bets was swarming with salmon, and the young Americans had often regretted not having brought fishing-tackle with them.

The ceremony of *Iyomante* lasted for nearly a week, during which time the Ainos freely indulged in *saké*. When the festival was over, the men went into the mountains to hunt ; and the women tilled the patches of grain, and split and wove the bark of a tree from which they make their clothing.

The bear's skin was duly cured and dried, then presented to Mrs. Jewett by Setta-eye.

"You cannot say you did not see it killed, mother," said Fitz. "I think you were entitled to its pelt."

The weather was delightfully mild up in the mountains; and the party were so pleased with Hokuyak-bets and its chief, that they lingered nearly a month in the place, every thing going on just as though they were not there.

Twice the Professor and boys went bear-hunting, and were rewarded by securing three fine *hokuyak*. As usual, Fitz enjoyed himself, and had an adventure which caused much merriment to his friends.

They had been hunting all the morning, and were resting and refreshing themselves with luncheon, when one of the dogs began to whimper as though he smelt a bear. The Ainos said it was a puppy, and did not know any thing; but that did not satisfy Fitz, who, hastily finishing his repast, ascended a rocky eminence, and, taking out a field-glass, began to scan the scenery.

"You will not see a trace of a bear," said his brother. "That dog gives tongue whenever it feels in the humor. Come down and take a rest while you have a chance."

"Sessch, sessch!" went Fitz, making a signal that he had discovered the game, and suddenly throwing himself upon his stomach.

The Professor regarded him with an amused expression, and said, —

"He will be tired out before night. See, he is levelling his weapon at something."

"He will hit it," said the young doctor. "Fitz is becoming a first-rate shot."

A puff of smoke came from the rifle, and they heard the ping of the bullet.

The young hunter put his glass to his eyes, and eagerly regarded something in the valley, then, cautioning his friends with his hand, reloaded and fired.

"I believe it is a bear," exclaimed the Professor. "Come, boys, let us join Fitz."

They grasped their rifles, and climbed up to the plateau; when Fitz said in a low tone, —

"I have hit him twice, but he don't budge. He is down there, between those two trees."

They levelled their glasses at the object, and simultaneously exclaimed, —

"Yes, it is a bear!"

In a few moments the whole party was blazing away like an old-fashioned target company.

"I saw it move its head," said Fitz.

"Suppose we try closer quarters," suggested the Professor, after the twentieth round. "I think the bear must have been shot through the heart."

Just then the Ainos — who had staid below in order to devour the remains of the lunch — joined them, and, on seeing the object of their attack, said, —

"The bear is dead!"

"I thought so," said Fitz, who had learned a few words of their language. "Come, let us go and examine my prize, and secure its skin."

"Your prize!" said Johnnie. "We all helped to kill him."

"Certainly we did," added his father. "I fired the shot that made it wag its head."

"I do not want to be too confident," remarked Oto; "but I believe my third shot settled the creature. I could see its eyes glistening, and I struck it in a vital spot."

"What are those Ainos grinning at?" said Fitz, in a somewhat annoyed tone.

"The bear is dead!" once more exclaimed the hunters.

"We know that," said Fitz; adding in English, "I do not like to be laughed at by savages."

The descent into the valley proved to be somewhat dangerous, and the party had several severe mishaps.

"I am afraid I have sprained my ankle," said the Professor. "This is very hard travelling."

"Better rest, sir," said the young doctor. "It is some distance to where the bear is lying. I will remain with you while the boys and hunters go and secure the skin."

The Professor and Oto seated themselves, and watched the lads.

They descended quite recklessly, and raced to see who should first examine the prize, finally reaching it almost simultaneously.

"What makes the Ainos laugh so?" queried the Professor. "My sons look as mad as hornets. Why, they are coming back without touching it!"

Neither of the lads hurried; and when they got within hailing distance, Oto shouted, —

"Was it not a bear?"

"Yes," grumbled Johnnie.

Not another word was spoken until they rejoined the party, when the Professor remarked, —

"I suppose the skin is shot all to pieces and quite useless."

Fitz, who could no longer contain himself, burst out laughing, and said, —

"The hunters were right when they said, 'The bear is dead.' It ceased to suffer a month ago."

They had great fun over this adventure; and, as the light was failing, made the best of their way home.

The next morning the Professor told the chief he must start for the north, on hearing which Setta-eye said,—

AINO WRESTLING WITH BEAR.

"Before you go, you should see one of my people wrestle with a bear which we captured last winter. It is a very clever animal, and understands every thing that is said to it."

The gentlemen of the party witnessed the exhibition, which took place in a large hut that served as a "city hall" for the tribe.

When the bear was led out of its cage, it was confronted by a hairy Aino, who, seizing it under and over its fore-arms, hugged it, and strove to lift it off the ground. After wrestling for a while, the shaggy brute rushed to the window, and, before the Ainos could prevent it, escaped through the aperture, and made for the mountains, followed in hot haste by the chief, his people, and about five hundred yellow dogs.

"Go it!" cried Fitz. "I hope the critter will get off. It is rough to be trotted out for wrestling-matches, and then squeezed to death and worshipped at *Iyomante*."

The chief did not return until nightfall, when he sorrowfully remarked to the Professor, —

"The bear has departed."

"We must go to-morrow," was the reply. "We shall never forget your hospitality."

Setta-eye saluted them in his courteous way, and, sighing, exclaimed, —

"Then my heart will be heavy. All one's friends leave at the same time."

CHAPTER IX.

" You, O sea, are our father, and you, forest, our mother : we humbly present our thanks to you both. Do not be jealous if we leave one to remain with the other.
"Our home is in the dense forests that lie in the heart of Yezo." — AINO'S SPEECH.

CHIEF SETTA-EYE was destined not to lose his guests for a while. The Professor's sprain, which the first day had appeared a trifling matter, prevented him from starting, and, indeed, threatened to keep him a prisoner at Hokuyak-bets.

"How long do you think it will be before I am fit to travel?" he inquired of Oto.

"Probably a fortnight," answered the young doctor. "Yesterday you walked from the mountain, then, instead of resting, went to see the man wrestle with the bear. The only thing is, to keep your foot from the ground, and to take matters easy."

"Well, I suppose I will have to do as you advise," said the Professor with a sigh. "While I am chained here, you and the boys had better visit Lake Kutzu-chako on the south-east, near Nemoro. Habo tells me a wonderful story of an Aino fort built on the top of a mound on the shore of the lake, the water of which never freezes. As I very much doubt that the Yezo-jin were ever smart enough to make a fortification, I would like you to go to the place. Perhaps you will find it is a dolmen or a hillock erected by mound-builders. Anyhow the trip will serve to while away the time."

They consulted the chief, who not only approved of the plan, but offered to accompany them.

The party consisted of Fitz, Johnnie, Oto, Setta-eye, Habo, and about fifty Ainos, who were armed with bows and poisoned arrows, and carried long spears.

"This is what I call having a good time," remarked Fitz. "We shall, no doubt, encounter a great many adventures."

The country was very mountainous, and on all sides they saw evidences of volcanic action.

After three days of exceedingly hard travel, they arrived at a plateau overlooking a beautiful lake.

"This is Kutzu-chako," said Habo; "and there, on the right, is Menka-koshi; that was made by the Ainos, and used as a place of retreat against their enemies."

The view was very beautiful. At their feet was the lake, on the blue waters of which rested a number of small craft, and far off rose the peaks of Mounts Meacan and Oakan.

"Those are extinct volcanoes," said Oto. "This whole island is dotted with such objects. See how red the sides look, as though the fires beneath them had just gone out."

The travellers descended into the village, and paid their respects to the officer of the Kaitakushi, who proved to be a very pleasant gentleman.

"I will take you to the old fort to-morrow," he remarked. "It is well worth visiting. Now rest yourselves, and enjoy my poor hospitality."

The official's house was surrounded by a stockade; but there was no gate at the entrance, or any sign that it was fortified against the Ainos.

The travellers were accommodated with nice rooms, and a mess of fresh fish was cooked for their supper.

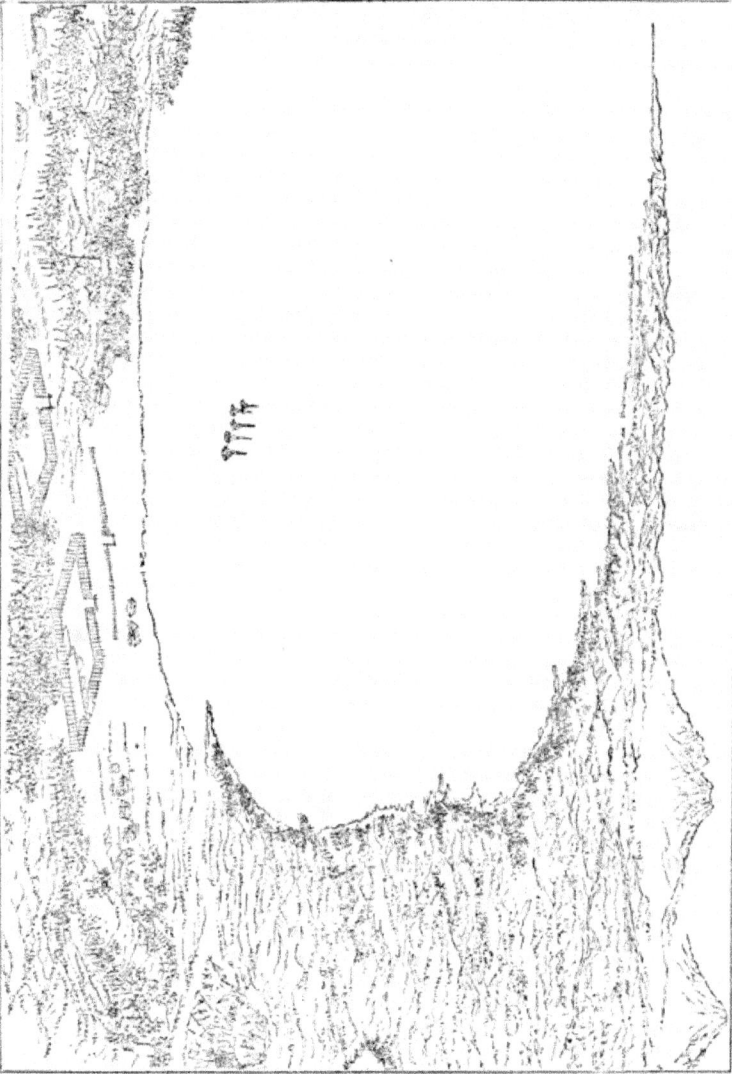

LAKE KUTZU-CHARO.

"There are quite a number of Japanese living here," remarked Johnnie. "One would scarcely think it paid them to settle in such an out-of-the-way place."

"We raise a great deal of wheat in this district," answered their host; "and the fishing of the lake is quite profitable."

Soon after the repast the boys begged permission to retire, saying they had not had a good night's rest since they left Hokuyak-bets.

At daybreak they were aroused by Habo, who said, —

"Come and see the Japanese catching *yabé*" (crayfish): "it is very amusing."

The boys hurried on their clothes, and ran down to the shore, where they saw a number of fishermen hauling a seine. There were about twenty adults in the party, and they were making noise enough for two hundred. When the net was dragged on to the beach, they emptied its contents into seine-shaped baskets of bamboo, then signalled the boats in the centre of the lake to approach and take the catch.

"Where do those craft come from?" inquired Johnnie.

"From Katsurakoi," Habo answered. "There the fish are put on board junks, and taken to Hakodate, where they are dried, and exported to China."

The boys watched the fishermen fill their baskets, and when the last crayfish was captured the lads returned to their host, the Japanese official. After breakfast, they started in a boat for Menka-koshi, a distance about three-quarters of a mile from their friend's residence.

The sun was very warm, and the air swarmed with enormous dragon-flies that flew hither and thither and made a whirring sound.

YABE (CRAYFISH) FISHING.

"We call those 'darning-needles' at home," said Fitz. "Have you ever seen them kill their prey?"

"What do they feed upon?" asked Oto. "I never saw them do any thing but fly from one rush to another."

"They hunt the daddy-longlegs," answered the boy. "I have watched them many a time. Poor old daddy would be sailing round enjoying himself, when along would come the dragon-fly; and in another instant the daddy would be lying headless on the veranda, and master dragon-fly would fly off, picking his teeth, and looking out for another victim."

"There is Menka-koshi," said their guide, pointing to a rocky hummock ahead of them. "We can sail all round it, but can only land in one place."

"I see there is a regular corduroy road built to the summit," said Johnnie. "I do not believe the Ainos ever made that."

Upon reaching the landing-place, they anchored the craft, went on shore, and began to ascend the road, which meandered spirally round the fort.

The steps were not made of timber, but were formed by splitting out layers of rock: this had evidently been done a long time ago, the pathway in some places being obstructed by large trees.

The travellers toiled along the ascent, and finally reached the top, which proved to be of solid rock, and as flat as a table.

"This was levelled by skilled masons," said Oto. "I believe it was made by the Japanese general, who centuries ago conquered some of the wild tribes in this part of Yezo. You see there are the marks of the chisels on this rock."

"I suppose this was fortified to command the lake," said Johnnie. "Even now it would be a good place on which to build a battery."

FORT MENKA-KOSHI.

The entire mound was a mass of granite, sparsely covered with black soil.

The Aino rose and wild honeysuckle illuminated the otherwise bare places, and clothed the mountain with a glory, the fragrance of which delighted the foreigners, and made even the natives sniff and exclaim, —

"*Pirika! Pirika!*" (good! good!)

"Menka-koshi, who was reported to have made this road, and to have fortified this hill, was a great chief," said Habo. "He was very tall, and as strong as a bear."

"He must have been, to have done what we see here," said Fitz. "My opinion is, that the story was made out of whole cloth. Down in Massachusetts we have rocks on which folks say Masconomo used to stand when he addressed his tribe. I do not believe old Masco ever went within five miles of some of them. It is very easy to invent a legend for a locality, and I guess that is what the Ainos have done in this case."

They returned to the settlement, and strolled round it, chatting with the Japanese; all of whom spoke as though they were in exile, and said they should be glad when they got back to their country.

"It is quite home-like to see nurse-girls walking about with children on their backs," said Oto. "One might almost fancy himself near Hakone."

As they were talking they heard a cry, —

"*Ah, honkewa Osaka Adzuchi machi Nobuyama kaden no senkintan!*"

("Patent thousand-gold medicine, the secret of which Nobuyama of Adzuchi Street, Osaka, has inherited.")

"*Hai!*" cried Johnnie. "What! are the *senkintan* men up here?"

They turned a corner, and beheld one of the most extraordinary sights they had seen in Yezo.

An old Aino, who had been drinking *saké* and offering *inaho* until he was overcome with the wine and religious observance, had been startled from his slumber by the cries of two sleek-looking Japanese, who, mounted on high clogs, were industriously visiting the settlers, in order to vend the celebrated patent nostrum known as *senkintan* (thousand-gold medicine). These indefatigable fellows swarm all over the empire, travel in couples, and chant the virtues of their panacea as follows :—

"*A-a, sono mata kusurino kono wa! A-a, dai-ichi hi-i wo totonoye, tan-seki, riuin, shiyoku-atari ; a-a, dzutsu to memai tachi-gurami ; a-a shoni mushibara-itami ni shiyoku-dzukaye.*"

("Oh! these are the properties of this medicine! It makes the stomach and the spleen strong. It is very good for hoarseness and colds, pyrosis, and the result of eating decayed food. It cures headache, giddiness, and dizziness on awakening, and is valuable for children's diseases.")

"What is the old man mad about?" inquired Fitz of Habo. "He is jabbering to that boy as though he were out of his mind."

The boy referred to was carrying three rods used by the Aino in a game played by throwing a hoop into the air and catching it on a stick.[1]

Habo listened to the conversation between her countrymen, then said,—

"The old gentleman is very pious, and has been making many *inaho* and drinking a great quantity of *saké*."

"Yes, he looks like it," said Fitz with a nod.

[1] *Vide* cover.

AN ANGRY AINO.

" He said," continued Habo, "'This is a very annoying thing. What do those Japanese mean by yelling in my ear when I am sleeping?' He hopped round in order to show his displeasure; and the boy laughed, and returned, 'Oh! those men sell a wonderful thing. It cures all diseases. You had better try some of it.'—'Foolishness! Foolishness!' replied the old fellow. 'There is only one medicine fit for an Aino, that is *saké.*'"

The *senkintan*-venders listened to the foregoing with amused faces, then turned, took opposite sides of the street, raised their umbrellas above their heads, and went off at a swinging trot, crying, —

" *Ah, honkewa Osaka Adzuchi machi Nobuyama kaden no senkintan !* "

" They beat every thing," said Oto. " Who ever expected to find *senkintan* men in this out-of-the-way place?"

" Where do they come from?" inquired Johnnie.

" From Osaka," said the young doctor. " A quack named Nobuyama concocted a mixture of starch, catechu, thuya, and licorice, which he flavored with elecampane, peppermint, cloves, and camphor, and made into little cakes divided into twenty portions, covered with tinfoil, each square being a dose. Minute directions accompany the package, and the article is used externally as well as internally. It has never been known to kill any one, and many people have imagined it has cured them of serious ailments. In order to advertise it, he hired hundreds of good-looking young men, and furnished them with a uniform consisting of handsome *kimono*" (coats), " oiled-paper cloaks, leggings, high clogs, and umbrellas bearing his sign, — two circles interlocked. Each man carries a little portmanteau decorated with the trade-mark. This receptacle contains several dozen packages of the *senkintan*. Twenty squares sell for ten cents, and forty for twenty. The pedlers chant their cry of '*A-a! honkewa Osaka*,' etc., and make poor

ignorant people curious to buy. Now, they say his emissaries have not only gone to China, but are thinking of proceeding to America and England."

"Well," remarked Fitz, "one more patent medicine won't hurt us. We shall have pictures of the inventor all over the country, with his signature in Japanese, and the legend, 'Yours for pelf, Nobuyama.' But, boys, do look at that old Aino!"

The savage had sunk upon his mat, seized a stick, and was whittling out an *inaho*, muttering as he did so, as though he could scarcely contain his anger; while far off, up the hillside, the boys heard the cry, —

"*Ah, honkewa Osaka Adzuchi machi Nobuyama kaden no senkintan!*"

The next day they started for Hokuyak-bets, and, after a weary journey in the rain, arrived at their Aino home. They found the Professor quite recovered from his accident, and ready to start for their long tramp through the mountain chain of North Yezo.

All useless articles were packed, and sent to Hakodate; and the travellers set out in light marching-order.

Chief Setta-eye and a number of his people accompanied them several miles upon the way, until they emerged upon a level plateau from which they had a grand view of Ishikari Mountain, one of the highest in Yezo.

When he prepared to take leave of them he wept, and said, —

"One does not know what there is in store for him. A short time ago I was ignorant of your existence, now my heart is heavy because I am about to part with you. Accept this poor present: it is all I have to give you."

After speaking, he waved his hands in his grand fashion, then abruptly turned and walked homeward, his people following him without adding a word. He had refused all offers of payment, and would not even take Fitz's watch, which the boy urged him to accept, and which must have been a great temptation to him.

The present he gave to the Professor proved to be a carved *saké*-stick, an object that few Ainos care to part with, and which the recipient treasures to this day.

"Mount Ishikari must have once been a volcano," said Johnnie, as they rested in a dry spot, and looked at the object referred to.

IN SIGHT OF MOUNT ISHIKARI.

"I believe it is now a reservoir," said Fitz, "and that it has burst. It seems to me, the Ainos follow the water-courses: we ought to have brought rubber-boots."

"It is no use grumbling, brother," said Sallie. "This scenery is wonderfully romantic. The gold, brown, green, purple, violet, blue, vermilion, and orange tones of the mountain peaks and spurs are perfectly glorious."

"Pooh!" said Fitz, "one would think you were describing a fashionable bonnet. For my part, I think the scene is horribly savage."

"What? With those telegraph-wires bisecting it?" she said. "No, brother, we are still within range of civilization, and cannot call this place savage with yonder signs of progress disfiguring the view."

"I suppose you would like to make the Japanese put them underground," muttered Fitz.

They saw several bears, and herds of deer, but did not meet with any adventure worth recording; their road lying in deep gorges and along hillsides overhanging terrific precipices. It was downright hard tramping, notwithstanding which Mrs. Jewett and Sallie were always to the fore, and kept the others in a good temper by their singing and cheerful demeanor.

They were fifteen days going from Hokuyak-bets to Daikotan, which proved to be a fishing-village inhabited by a mixed population of Japanese and Aino.

The Professor expected to meet the man-of-war; but the ship had not arrived, so they had to put up with somewhat rough accommodation, and amuse themselves as best they could.

One day they took a boat, and went out to see the *shibé* (bonito) fishing. A great number of craft had surrounded a school of *shibé*, and driven it into a huge net, the floats of which were made of long poles, of a peculiar kind of pine as light as cork.

The scene was very exciting, — the fishermen securing the bonito with their boat-hooks, and throwing them kicking and squirming into the bottoms of their boats. Sometimes a huge fish would spring clear out of the water; and many of them leaped the floats, and regained their freedom.

After waiting several days at Daikotan, the travellers started for Soya on the western coast of Yezo, where they had an

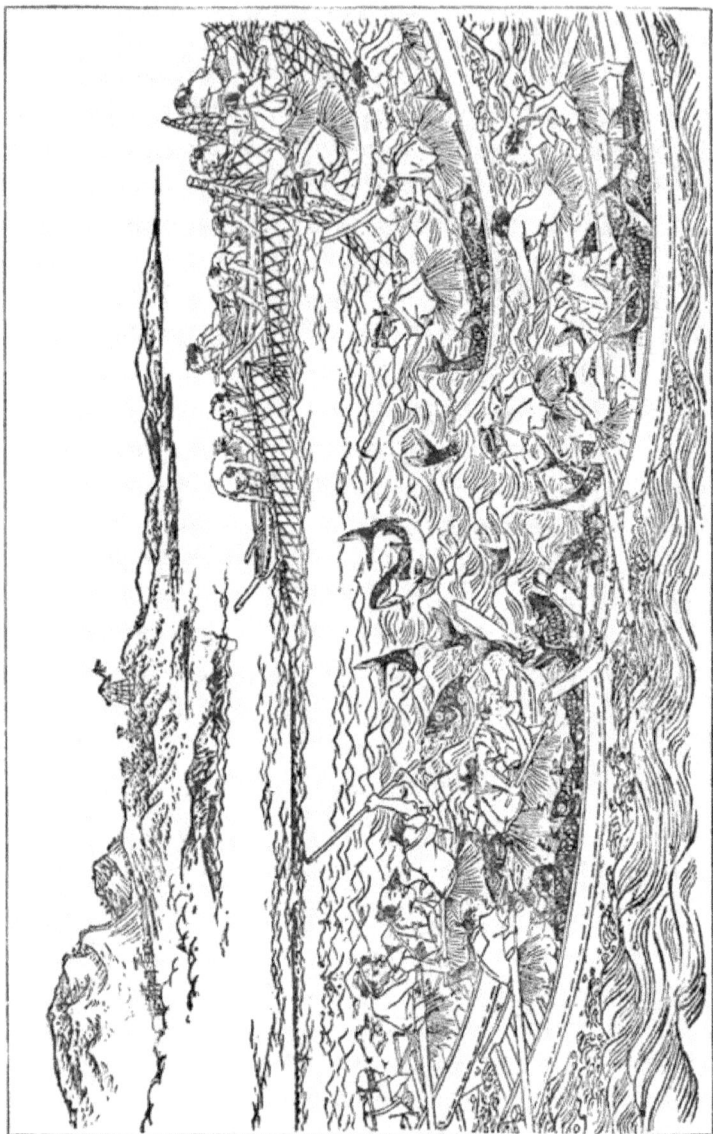

SHIBÉ (BONITO) FISHING.

opportunity of witnessing the Ainos hunting seals. The men speared the fish just as they had done in the south; but the seals proved to be much larger, and had a peculiar formation on the ends of their tails. This the Professor pronounced to be the result of a disease. The Aino called them *onetsufu*, and they were between six and seven feet long.

NORTHERN SEAL.

There was a Japanese artist staying at Soya, who gave the young Americans some very clever sketches he had made of the manners and customs of the Yezo-jin. One represented a party of fishermen setting out to capture seals in the winter. In the foreground were three mats, two of which were occupied by men making *inaho*. A woman was passing a spear out of the window of a snow-covered hut, and her husband was receiving it, while another Aino was evidently joking with them. Three fishermen were preparing the boat for launching, and were raising their hands as though pointing to seals upon the ocean.

"These will be nice to show to our friends at home," said Sallie.

On the second morning of their stay at Soya, Habo awoke them in great haste, saying, —

"Please rise. The man-of-war is in port, and the boat will soon come on shore. To-day you will be able to start for Hakotan in the island of Karafuto."

They rose quickly, and, before they were dressed, heard Capt. Imadate saying, —

"Where are you all? I am anxious to remove you from this savage country."

"Here we are," cried Fitz, putting his head out of the window. "We have had a splendid time, — used to rise at one o'clock in the morning, lived among the Ainos, went bear-hunting, and were hunted in return, and saw them kill and worship the *kami hokuyak.*"

The whole party then quitted the hut, and welcomed the captain, who said, —

"It is really wonderful that you are all alive. I have lots of letters for you, and some telegrams from Tokio. Come on board, and enjoy a good breakfast."

After they had chatted a while with their friend, the three Aino chiefs, who had been their guides, advanced with Habo, and said through her, —

"We have now delivered you safely into the hands of the government officials: nothing remains for us but to say *saramba*" (good-by). "May you have a very pleasant journey, and return safely to your native place ! "

Having thus spoken they clasped their hands, then raised

AINO SEAL-HUNTERS.

them to the tops of their heads, and gradually brought them downward; as they did so, uttering their strange, dog-like cry.

"They are only animals anyhow," said Capt. Imadate, contemptuously regarding the guides, who were shedding tears.

"No," answered Mrs. Jewett: "they are men, with gentle, kindly natures, and warm hearts. What can we do, captain, to reward these good people?"

"I will send them a tub of *saké*," he answered. "That will make them perfectly happy."

"I would prefer to give them a barrel of sugar," said the lady.

"Just as you say, madam," answered the captain.

Habo was paid a gratuity; and the old fellows received their reward, which they promised to share with Setta-eye.

The last the Jewetts saw of their guides was the latter ascending the mountains, homeward bound: the men carrying between them the barrel of sugar, slung on a bearing-pole, and Habo weeping like a child.

"Yes," said Fitz. "Mother was right: all the world likes candy."

The travellers embarked on board the man-of-war, where they found a Russian officer, who had been sent by his government to acts as interpreter to the party.

In half an hour they were steaming across the strait called by foreigners La Pérouse, in honor of the great navigator of that name.

CHAPTER X.

KARAFUTO (SAGHALIN).

*" Many so-called savages are much more gentle and noble than the mass of
people who are termed civilized. Among the former are to be classed the five tribes
that inhabit the island of Karafuto; viz., the Aino, the Samelenko, the Oroko, the
Colletské, and the Santan."* — MEMOIRS OF LA PÉROUSE.

THE Russian interpreter (Lieut. Ivan Koski) was, like
many of his countrymen, an accomplished English scholar :
he therefore proved a valuable addition to the party.

As the ship steamed across the strait, he said to the Professor, —

" You will find the natives of this island very different from
those of Yezo. Of course you are aware that in 1875 Saghalin, or, as the natives call it, Karafuto, was ceded to us in return
for the Kurile Islands, which are valuable for fishing-stations.
There has been a great deal written and said about our forcing
Japan to make the exchange, while the truth is, the benefit was
mutual. We have long desired to have a refuge for our ships
off the coast of Tartary, and Japan has wished to have a legal
title in the Kurile Islands ; besides which, out of the twenty-
three hundred natives in Karafuto, only a very few on the west
coast are Aino, the others being the Samelenko who live on
the western side, the Santan and Colletské who occupy the
extreme north and who wander all over the country, and the
Oroko who inhabit the eastern shore. The centre of the island
is a chain of mountains, only visited by the natives when hunt-

ing. I have been stationed here for three years, and have made a study of the habits and customs of the people."

While they were chatting, Capt. Imadate approached, and bowing said, —

"The current runs at terrific speed through this strait. Though it is only thirty-eight miles, as the crow flies, to Hakotan, we shall travel twice that distance before we make the harbor. Have you read your letters yet, Professor?"

"Yes," answered the gentleman. "I am exceedingly gratified with the communication from Tokio. I am requested to make a report on the condition of the Ainos who remain in Karafuto. It is very pleasant to know that the Russian Government has not only agreed to my doing this for Japan, but has detailed Lieut. Koski to accompany us."

They conversed until dinner-time, then descended to the cabin, and, for the first time in many weeks, enjoyed a meal cooked in American fashion.

Fitz could scarcely contain his delight when he saw a loaf of bread; and, upon the ice-cream being served, he nudged Oto, and whispered, —

"Isn't this *ichi-ban!*" (number one.)

It was about seven o'clock when they steamed into Hakotan Bay, a small harbor on the south-western shore of Karafuto.

"There is our flag!" exclaimed Lieut. Koski, pointing to the right. "That building is the Government House. I hope you will land, and be my guests until we leave here."

The Professor accepted his hospitality; and that night the party slept on Russian beds, placed upon flues that ran through the centre of the chambers.

At sunrise they looked across the water, and saw the Cape of Shiranoshi.

"We tried to make a settlement there about twenty-eight years ago," said the lieutenant, "but it was a failure. At that time we were at war with England and France, and the ships of those nations swarmed in these waters. When we acquired Saghalin, we placed officials in all the principal ports, appointed a governor, worked the coal, and utilized the island as a penal settlement."

"Don't the natives object to that?" inquired Fitz.

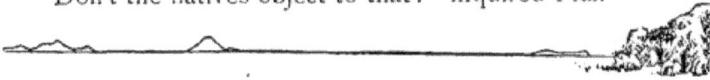

HAKOTAN BAY.

"We have never asked them," said the officer. "On our taking possession, nearly all the Ainos went to Sapporo in Yezo; and those that remained are, as you will see, more like Tartars. Here come my servants."

He pointed to two native girls who were returning from market, carrying neat baskets made of birch-bark. Their mouths and hands were not tattooed, and their faces were very unlike those of the Ainos of Yezo. Their costumes were different, being of Japanese cotton and of deer-skin, ornamented with brass buttons. They wore leggings of bear-skin, and high boots that reached to their knees.

" I see they comb their hair," said Sallie, " and wear double earrings. Indeed, they are entirely different from the people whom we have hereto seen."

Mrs. Jewett was much interested in the girls, and put many questions to the interpreter.

AINO GIRLS. (KARAFUTO).

They invited the ladies to visit the kitchen, and showed them a Russian cooking-stove, in which they evidently took great pride.

" What are those garments hanging on poles?" asked Fitz, who had followed his mother and sister.

"Those are our winter furs and belts," replied one of the girls. "We suspend our clothes in the smoke to preserve them. The brass ornaments and buttons for our dresses and belts are bought in Tartary: we get them from the Samelenko."

"They wear high-necked dresses with funnel-shaped sleeves," said Fitz. "It appears to me that these Karafuto Ainos have a good deal more style about them than the Yezo-jin."

The ship remained one day at Hakotan, then started at sunrise

AINO GIRL'S GIRDLE.

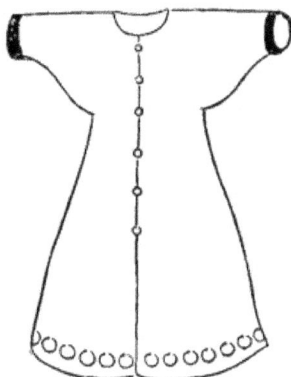

AINO GIRL'S DRESS.

for Kogoho, where the Ainos were going to hunt bears.

Kogoho was about two miles and a half from Shiranoshi, and proved to be a mere open roadstead.

The gentlemen of the party landed in the whale-boat, and visited the fort, which was a most interesting relic of an ancient race. The walls were well built of very large stones, and formed three sides of a hollow square; the front being guarded by a portion of the rock on which the fort was erected.

"What pains they must have taken to construct this!" remarked Johnnie. "Why, they have actually cut a moat out of the solid rock on the three sides of the wall!"

"Yes; and it is deep too," said Fitz. "This was never made by Ainos."

"That is my opinion," remarked Oto.

" What do you think, lieutenant ? " inquired the Professor.

" That it was made by Tartars. . I believe at one time this island belonged to Tartary."

While they were conversing, two men and a boy approached them, and asked if they would like to go bear-hunting. The men were middle-aged, and were clothed in skin robes, more or less ornamented with brass. Unlike the Yezo Ainos, they wore boots and leggings ; and their hair was not shaggy, and bore

KOSOHO   ANCIENT FORT.

marks of the comb. The boy was simply costumed in a bear-skin coat, and carried a fish-spear.

" There is a bear up in the mountains," said the elder of the hunters, who was armed with a bow and arrows. " His retreat is not far from here."

As the travellers had their rifles with them, they decided to accept the invitation.

After climbing some high rocks, they found themselves in some " bad land " sparsely covered with gnarled and dwarfed trees.

The climate of Karafuto is, in summer, very dry; and the dead leaves do not decay, as in some countries, but accumulate in holes and recesses where they mat into peat-like layers that are perfect pitfalls to the unwary.

Fitz sank nearly up to his chest in a hole, the surface of which looked like the surrounding ground. The Ainos laughed

AINO HUNTERS (KARAFUTO).

at his mishap, and lifted him out; at the same time informing their visitors that sometimes people had altogether disappeared in such hollows, and were smothered.

"I believe that one goes right through to the West Indies," said the merry boy. "After this I am going to be cautious where I step."

They found the bear in the hands of six Ainos, who, while their friends had gone, had contrived to drive the brute into a pitfall, and to capture it alive. When they first saw the creature it was being carried by four Ainos, who had fastened its limbs to stout saplings and tied a hide rope round its neck. In conveying the poor beast, it hung head downwards; and it was evidently suffering great pain.

Upon beholding the travellers they deposited their burden right side up on the ground, and sat upon the ends of the poles, in order to keep it from moving.

"What are you going to do with it?" inquired the lieutenant.

The chief hunter saluted, and replied, —

"We were told that some foreign gentlemen were coming here to hunt bears. As it is very difficult to find them just when you want to do so, we thought we would capture this alive, and bring it down to the fort, so that the strangers could shoot it at their leisure."

As he spoke, he thrust a stick between the jaws of the bear to rouse the animal from its lethargy.

The Professor said his party did not desire to hunt in that fashion; hearing which, the second hunter grasped the animal by the ears, and the chief proceeded to saw off its teeth in order to keep it from injuring people, it being destined for sacrifice at the festival of *Iyomante*.

The foreigners entered a hut which was built much after the fashion of those in Yezo. Over the fire was a large iron pot filled with bear-flesh broth, flavored with various herbs that gave out a medicinal odor. One of the women dished this mess in a wooden vessel that had two ear-like handles decorated with the conventional wave pattern.

"Are they going to ask us to chip in and take tiffin with them?" whispered Fitz to the lieutenant. "I don't hanker after such diet."

PREPARING A BEAR FOR CAPTIVITY.

"It is really very good when you are used to it," replied the Russian. "See, they are bringing in their dogs to enjoy the meal."

At that moment two girls entered with puppies on their backs. It was comical to see the little things play with their attendants' earrings, and to hear the girls address them as they would children.

The Professor, who always enjoyed novel entertainments, seated himself on the matted floor, and said to his sons, —

"Now, boys, try and eat for the sake of politeness. Nothing

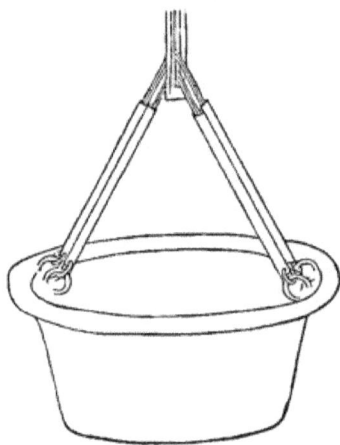

COOKING POT.

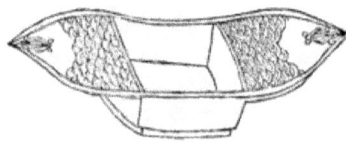

WOOD BOWL FOR FOOD.

pleases a host so much as to find his guests partaking freely of what has been provided for them. Although this stew smells rather herby, I have no doubt it tastes good."

The boys did not "enthuse much," and, when they were served, placed their bowls of food upon the ground, and encouraged the puppies to approach them. The Ainos ate their food with *hashi* (chop-sticks), and made a great noise over the process.

The Professor manfully attacked his portion, and, after emptying his bowl, put it forward for a second helping; as he did so, beaming upon their host, and saying to the lieutenant, —

"Tell them I consider it very good. I admire the Same-lenko, and I enjoy this soup."

After a while his chopsticks moved slower and slower, he began to examine his food suspiciously, and finally he hurriedly rose, and quitted the hut, followed by his sons and Oto.

"What is the matter, sir?" inquired the latter, while Johnnie and Fitz regarded their parent with great anxiety.

He motioned the boys not to follow him, and when he rejoined them he was exceedingly quiet.

"What is the matter?" inquired Lieut. Koski, who just then came out of the hut, wiping his lips as though he had enjoyed his repast. "Was the food too much for you?"

"Yes, it was," frankly answered the gentleman. "The atmosphere of the hut was very close, and I must say the ingredients of the stew were somewhat startling." Then turning to his sons he continued, "You appear to have liked it, boys."

Fitz looked slyly at his brother, noticing which his father demanded, —

"Well, sir, what amuses you?"

DOGS' NURSES.

"We ate ours by proxy, sir," demurely answered the boy. "I could not bring myself to touch any of that composition."

"It was a rash act on my part," said the Professor. "I suppose after a while one might get used to such diet, but my first experience has not been encouraging."

They returned to the shore, and, embarking on board the man-of-war, steamed along the coast; which presented a succession of rocky views, and proved the lieutenant's assertion that the island was a mountain chain.

They anchored for a few hours at Kushunai, a good harbor, one hundred and eighty miles from Hakotan. They saw in the distance an extinct volcano, which the lieutenant informed them was called Horonobori, and was situated on the other side of the island.

"We will visit it when we descend the eastern coast," said Capt. Imadate. "Kushunai is a famous place for raising sleigh-dogs. Would you like to go on shore? There are no Ainos living to the north of this."

The ladies asked if they could accompany the party; and, upon being answered in the affirmative, they embarked in the ship's boat, and landed at the village, which was alive with dogs of all sizes and colors, and whose whining, yelping, and barking were deafening. Near every house was a hitching-post to which were tied a number of young animals, who tugged at their hide-ropes, and growled savagely at the Americans.

"Why are those puppies fastened, while the big dogs have their liberty?" asked Sallie.

"They are being taught to work," replied the Russian. "The Ainos tie them to a bob-sled, which they place near some dried fish, that has been toasted to develop the odor: as soon as the puppies smell this, they tug and tug until they reach it, when the trainer rewards them with a few morsels of the food. The distance between the sled and fish is increased every day; until finally they are taken several miles off, when, if they run home swiftly, they are well fed, and pronounced broken in, after which they have their freedom like adult dogs."

The visitors saw a woman feeding some puppies with dried hake and scraps of deer-fat. When they ate too fast she rapped them on the nose with a wooden spatula, and talked to them as though they were children.

"What a loud-pattern *kimono*" (coat) "that Aino wears!" said Fitz. "From whence do they get their cotton cloth?"

TRAINING SLEIGH-DOGS.

"From Tartary," said the lieutenant. "They manufacture a cloth of a grass called *mostie*, which they bleach in the sun, then weave into a fabric termed *tedrabe*. It looks like Russian linen."

"Don't they make any clothes of bark-fibre?" inquired Fitz.

"A few," was the reply: "however, the greater number of the garments are made of *tedrabe*."

"That poor little boy leading the dog is blind, is he not?" remarked Sallie.

"The puppy is leading him," answered the lieutenant. "He lost his sight through having varioloid. I believe the disease will ultimately exterminate these tribes."

About four o'clock the travellers re-embarked on board the man-of-war, which steamed northward for Kitoshi, — a place famous for its mountain. They sighted the latter about sunset, and had a charming view of it, illuminated with the rays of the setting orb.

"How glorious!" exclaimed Sallie, clasping her hands.

"Yes," said Fitz, imitating her manner, — "lemon-colored peaks trimmed with orange, vermilion, and brown, with a gold ruche: that is the way you will describe it, is it not, Sallie?"

"No, I shall not," she indignantly replied. "You do not appreciate color-harmony."

They passed close into the shore, and could see millions of glittering spots in the streams that descended both sides of the mountain.

"Those are salmon," said the lieutenant. "The Samelenko come down here, and spear great numbers of them. Farther up, the stream widens; and we have established a cannery, run by exiles."

"What!" said Sallie. "Do Russians live here?"

The lieutenant smiled, and replied, —

"Oh, yes! Some of our people are not satisfied with the government, and have tried to assassinate our emperor: so they have been sent hither to earn an honest living."

"But don't they freeze to death during the winter?" exclaimed the horrified girl.

"A few of them do," was the nonchalant reply. "If they had not been so savage, they would have remained at home. I have no pity for such people."

MOUNT KITOSHI.

That evening they anchored in the harbor of Kitoshi, where they had to be carried on shore, on account of the tide being low, and the water very shallow.

As they landed they saw a Samelenko standing on the shore, watching their approach. He had just rolled up a net, and secured it between some stakes, when he caught sight of the strangers.

"Why, he wears his hair in a tail, almost like a Chinese," said Fitz.

"Yes," said the lieutenant. "The Karafuto Ainos are a mixture of Samelenko and Yezo-jin ; while the Colletské, Oroko, and Santan are probably portions of Tartar tribes who have crossed from the continent."

"What continent?" inquired Johnnie.

"Tartary, over there," answered the lieutenant.

The Samelenko, who had somewhat recovered from his astonishment, approached, and, quieting his dog with a gesture of his hand, asked what he could do for the strangers.

The officer told him the travellers were from a very distant land, and that they desired to learn how the Samelenko lived, and to see their country. This puzzled the man, who, after thinking a while, replied, —

"I do not understand your motive : however, you can see all you want to, only do not hurt any of our people. You can go wherever you like, but must look out for poisoned arrows and fox-traps."

A tent was sent on shore ; and that night the party slept under canvas, and enjoyed a good rest on Samelenko land.

SAMELENKO MAN.

CHAPTER XI.

AMONG THE SAMELENKO.

"Woman was the last created, and is therefore the most perfect being. Although she may commit any sin, it is not right to put her to death." — SAME-LENKO PROVERB.

THE next morning the travellers were up betimes, they hearing the natives in earnest conversation outside their tent.

"Come and see Barnum's show," said Fitz. "Here is a girl with a bear on her back, and a hunter in a fancy hat. How curiously they dress their hair! One has it braided, and another wears a pug; and, O Sallie! do look at their earrings."

The man in the hat proved to be a chief, who had been hunting in the mountains, and had captured a young bear, which his wife was carrying on her back.

The lieutenant invited them to approach, then inquired where they had found the cub.

"Up in the Kitoshi Mountain," answered the chief, who wore a sealskin hunting-coat, marked with peculiar white spots. "I killed the mother, and brought this little thing down to bring up until he is big enough to sacrifice."

"These Samelenko worship the bear," said Lieut. Koski. "They look like Tartars, but have many Aino ways. Do you notice that woman carrying her child in a cradle? Poor little wretches, their hands are bound, and they can only move their feet. When a woman is tired of nursing her child, she hangs

SAMELE/NKOS

it up from a beam in her hut. Would you like to see one of their winter residences?"

"Not till after breakfast, thank you," said the Professor. "They might wish us to take a meal with them."

"The Samelenko speak a different language from the Ainos, do they not?" asked Johnnie.

"Very different," was the response. "And they can scarcely understand the Oroko, Colletské, or Santan dialects.

SAMELENKO HAT AND PILLOW.

You see, these people must have come from Tartary. They dress like Northern Chinese, and, unlike the Ainos, wear hats. Before we took possession of this island, the four tribes used to laugh at the Ainos, because they were subjects to the Emperor of Japan; the Samelenko, Colletské, Santan, and Oroko tribes always professing to be Tartar subjects. The women are really very clever and bright, and are so much esteemed by the men that they never put them to death. They are good tailors, make all the garments, and those hats you see the men wear."

"Of what are they made?" inquired Fitz.

"Of *kaba*-bark split into threads, and stiffened after it is woven. The chiefs are very proud of those head-dresses, which can be folded up and carried in the bosom when not required for use. The women also make the long Chinese pillows, which are covered with cotton. Altogether, a Samelenko woman's position is not a bad one."

"Do they ever bathe?" inquired Johnnie.

"I believe they wash their hands and faces every day,"

OUTSIDE OF UNDERGROUND HOUSE.

answered their friend; "though, as a rule, a little water goes a long way with them."

"Come, boys," said Sallie, "breakfast is ready. I am anxious to get it over, and go and see the Samelenko in their homes."

The meal was soon despatched, and at its conclusion the party set out to inspect the village.

Nearly all the houses were well built, and showed a knowl-

edge of carpentery which the travellers had never seen among
the Ainos. There was an air of neatness about the dwellings,
and in some an attempt at decoration.

"That is an underground house," said their guide, pointing
to what looked like some roughly trimmed timbers resting on

INSIDE OF UNDERGROUND HOUSE.

the top of a mound, in front of which was a sort of archway
made of saplings.

"You do not mean to say people live in that hole?"
queried Johnnie.

"Yes," was the reply. "It is intensely cold here in winter:
so the natives select a hillock, like this one, and excavate a
chamber in it, then cut a chimney in the centre of the roof, and
cover it with timbers or bark. During five months of the year

these habitations are buried in snow; but even then, and spite of the severe frosts, they are warm and comfortable, while in summer they are cool retreats. Come and see how cosey they are inside."

They entered, and found themselves in a square apartment lined with wood, stained brown with smoke, but very neatly kept. A high bench, covered with thick mats, extended round three sides of the apartment.

The fireplace was a wooden frame, filled with ashes, set in the centre of the floor; and on it was a large iron vessel containing water; and suspended by an iron rod from the beam was the only cooking-utensil, a huge kettle holding about ten gallons.

A sort of double sideboard supported sundry dishes, bowls, and wooden platters, attached to which was a box containing spoons, chop-sticks, and knives, and a wooden sieve for cleaning grain.

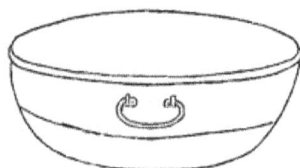
IRON COOKING-POT.

The Professor examined the cooking-utensils, and remarked, — "These forms are very ancient; the vessels appear to be made of hammered metal."

"They all come from Tartary," said their guide. "I do not think there are a dozen Japanese articles in use among these people."

"They have no *inaho*," remarked Fitz. "Their heads are level. The Yezo-jin spend half their time whittling god-sticks. Do the Samelenko drink *saké?*"

"They will drink any thing," was the answer. "They think whatever foreign stuff comes in bottles must be good. I know of a case where a whaling captain sold them a box

of aniline dyes, which they drank without any serious conse-
quences."

"Why, there is a *samisen*," (1) said Sallie, "and some stone
pipes" (3).

"That instrument came from Tartary. Its head is covered
with snake's-skin. They play it with an ivory picker (2).

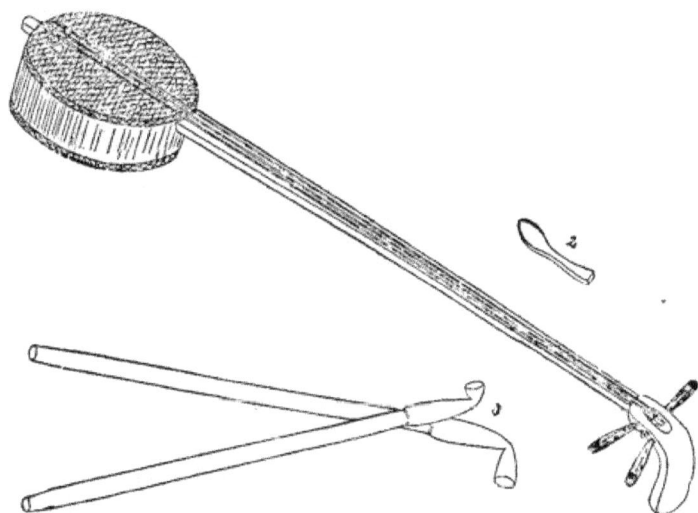

SAMELENKO GUITAR AND PIPES.

The pipes are made of red stone, something like those carved
by your Indians."

There being little more to interest them in the underground
dwelling, they took their leave, and strolled on to the beach,
where they found a native repairing a canoe, which was hauled
up beyond the tide-mark.

"These craft are made by the Colletské," said the Russian.
"They are the boat-builders of the island. If you notice, there
are bone spikes instead of thole-pins; and no metal is used

in the construction of the canoes, which are flat-bottomed, and quite square in the stern. The natives only quit the shore in calm weather, and these craft are pulled or sailed to and from the coast of Tartary."

Fitz critically examined the canoe, then said, —

" This is a regular coffin.   What are the sails made of?"

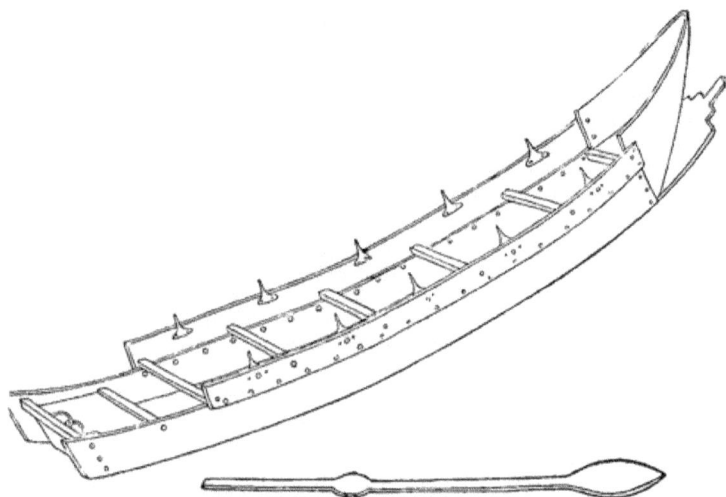

BOAT MADE BY COLLETSKÉ.

" Of fish-skin," replied their friend.   " They are worth a great deal to these poor people."

At the request of the officer, the fisherman fetched a sail, which he unrolled for their inspection.

" What fishes are these taken from?" asked Johnnie.

" Skates," was the reply.   " They grow to an enormous size in these waters, and their skins are very tough."

" I see they make the sculls spoon-shaped," said Fitz. " There is a hole bored through the swell near the handle.   I wonder how they hit upon that idea."

" I suppose they bought their experience by practice," re-marked his father. " These people have no science."

" Here comes our boat," said Sallie. " I see the sailors have taken down the tent."

" Yes," said Capt. Imadate, who just then joined them : " we start for Wakee as soon as you get on board. You will probably land there to-night."

The Japanese sailors were very handy, and had packed every thing neatly.

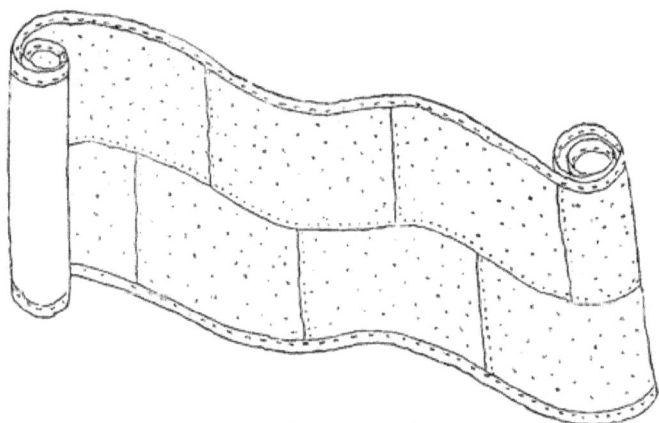

SAIL MADE OF FISH-SKIN

" I do so dislike being carried !" said Sallie : " it seems too bad to be treated like a child."

" Well, you can neither wade nor swim here," said Fitz, who was mounted on the back of a Japanese sailor. " If you are so awfully squeamish, you ought to stay on board."

His sister bit her lips, but did not make any further remarks.

Upon reaching the vessel, the anchor was tripped ; and they proceeded along the coast, passing a place called Natuko, off which they saw a number of boats fishing.

The water being somewhat rough, it took longer than the captain expected to reach Wakee: so the travellers determined to stay on board all night.

On landing the next morning, they were much tormented with flies and mosquitoes, which "fell upon the travellers," and almost drove them frantic: however, about noon a sea-breeze sprang up, and soon increased to quite a gale. This cooled the air, and carried the insect-pests towards the mountains.

Wakee is only two miles and a half from Otsutaka-baaha, on the coast of Tartary; but, as the water rushes through the strait at a tremendous pace, the passage is exceedingly dangerous. The natives said, that at very low tide they could walk from Wakee to the opposite shore, and that in winter, when the strait was frozen, they went backwards and forwards in their dog-sleds.

The visitors strolled about while their tent was being pitched, and presently came to a place where some millet was growing among a lot of high grasses that almost choked the crop. Two Samelenko were watching it, and a bird-rattle they had just erected to keep off the sparrows.

One of them was dressed in a sealskin coat and *kaba*-bark pants, and the other in deerskin.

"Is not their hair slicked down!" said Fitz. "I believe they wet it before they use a comb."

As he spoke, a girl came by, carrying a load of wood on her back; on seeing whom, another girl, who had been gathering a sort of wild grass for greens, called to her, —

"Have you seen the savages?" (meaning the Americans.)

When this was translated to the party, they laughed until their sides ached; and presently the Professor exclaimed, —

"I wonder what that young lady considers civilization?"

"I know, sir," said Fitz.   "Her idea of a fine costume is a tanned deerhide dress, trimmed with pieces of stamped brass, bearskin leggings, cowhide boots, window-curtain earrings, and a load of wood that would tax the endurance of a mule.   She evidently does not take much stock in us."

When the tent was pitched, the ladies retired to take a little rest, and the gentlemen went for a walk in the country.

WAKEE GIRLS.

They found the land rocky and full of rivulets, across which were laid pieces of drift-wood and portions of trunks of trees that served as bridges.   Nearly all of these were surmounted by otter-traps, those animals being a great annoyance to the Samelenko.   In one place they found a salmon caught fast in the noose intended for the otter.

"How is this?" said Johnnie.   "The fish was not taking a walk?"

"Certainly not," answered the lieutenant.   "An otter had captured the salmon, and was crossing this timber, when it sprung the trap.   Probably the head of the fish was in the noose, and the springing of the bow jerked it out of its captor's mouth."

As they advanced they saw many traps, and in one place

beheld a fox gazing wistfully at two dried perch attached to the trunk of a tree. The beast was so intent upon the tempting bait that he did not notice the intruders, or that there was a trap among the grass within a yard of his tail. After making two attempts to climb the tree he backed, as though preparing to take a run, and touching the trap was caught by the tail, and

HOINU. OTTER-TRAP.

swung high in the air; whereupon a native boy, who had followed the party, advanced, and killed the poor animal.

There was very little to interest the visitors in the place; and, when the wind ceased to blow, the mosquitoes and flies returned in such numbers that Mrs. Jewett declined to stay on shore.

"There are fewer insects at Hokobi," said Capt. Imadate.

"I was afraid you would not be able to stay here. This spot is quite famous for these pests."

"Infamous, you mean, captain," suggested Fitz. "Mother seldom complains, as you know. Things must be unendurable to make her grumble."

"I have another reason for going," said the captain. "I

SAMELENKO FOX-TRAP.

want to reach Hokobi before dark. The rocks there extend almost across to Tartary, and I would like to pass them during daylight."

As soon as they reached the ship the latter started, and in two hours approached the passage between Hokobi and the main land. It was, as the captain had said, very narrow; and, although the tide was high, the ship bumped perceptibly.

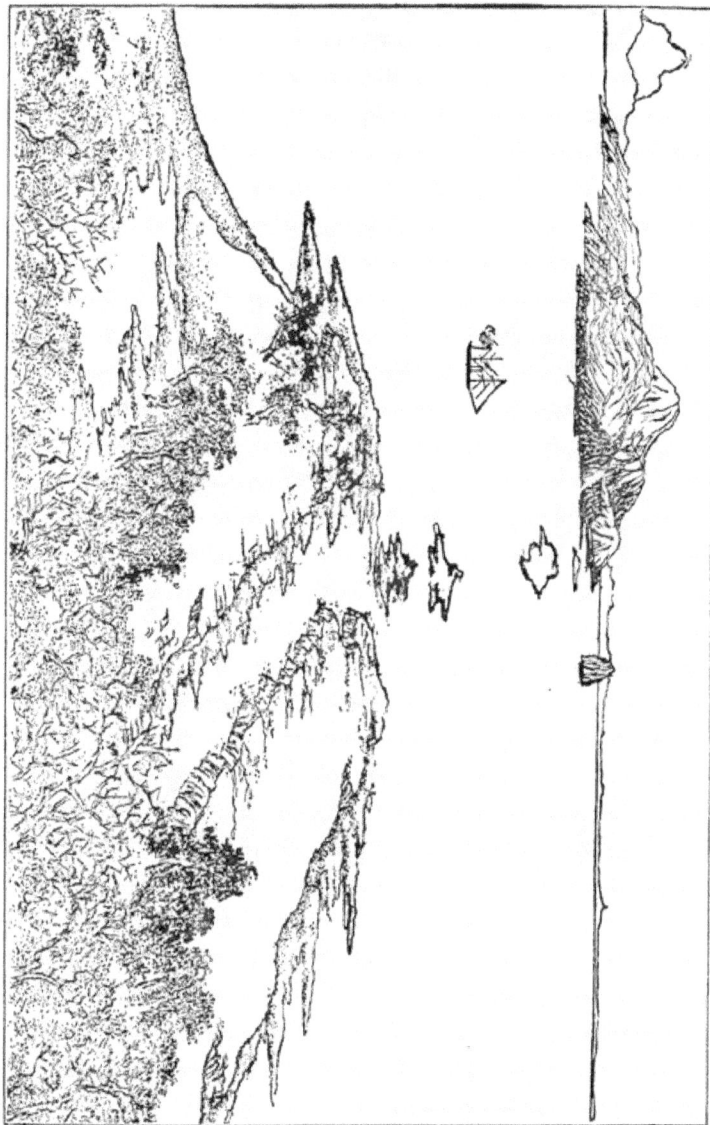

They steamed into a little inlet, like a dock ; and the party remained on board until the morning, when they landed, and visited the village.

The Samelenko were very hospitable, and invited them into their huts, in one of which a young woman dressed in a cotton

SAMELENKO LADY AT HER TOILET.

robe, lavishly decorated with tufts of cord and brass ornaments, was making her toilet. She used no bowl, but bent over a birch-bark basket filled with water. Having taken a mouthful of this, she squirted some of it on a huge wooden comb, then ran the latter through her luxuriant hair, repeating the operation until her tresses were straightened out, when she smiled sweetly, and proceeded to braid them.

"Have they no looking-glasses?" inquired Sallie.

"They possess some few Chinese ones, made of metal," replied the lieutenant; "but they do not use them very much, as they consider it is unlucky to see their own image."

"What is yonder funny-looking thing on the shelf?" inquired Fitz.

"That is the house-god," said the lieutenant.

"He is a sweet bird, is he not?" murmured Fitz. "What

SAMELE KO GOD AND GOD-HOUSE.

a lovely mouth he has! It is the nearest approach to an idol I have seen since I left Japan. I suppose that little wooden house is intended for his residence."

The owner of the image replied in the affirmative, and made an apology for the unfinished state of the image, saying, —

"I broke my knife yesterday, when I was carving that;" adding, in a complacent manner, "if you come in a day or two, I will have it finished and put in the god-house."

"Please tell him not to hurry on our account," said Johnnie.

"It is about the worst attempt at carving we have met with. Ask him whom it is intended to represent."

When this question was put to the man, he appeared to be puzzled, and finally owned that he did not know; then changed the conversation by saying, —

"Would you like to see my storehouse?"

"Certainly," said the Professor.

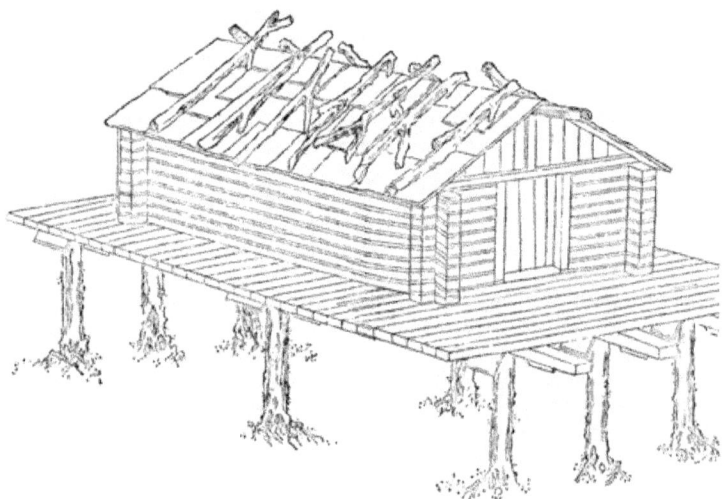

SAMELENKO STOREHOUSE.

The Samelenko led the way to the rear of his dwelling, and pointed to a structure made of finished planks, mounted upon tree-stumps; saying, —

"It is very hard to dig holes in the ground here: so I selected a spot where the trees were thick, cut them off at one height, and placed cross-timbers on them. Then the Colletské men brought their tools, and built my *noro* for me. You see, the arched pieces of bark, laid on the tops of the stumps, are to prevent the rats and mice from ascending to the platform."

"Why do they put such heavy timbers on the shingles?" inquired Sallie.

"To keep them from being blown away, miss," answered their guide. "The old chief wishes to know whether you would like to see some of his treasures."

"Certainly," replied the Professor. "Has he any valuable curios?"

The man unfastened the door by pushing up the panel, then lifted out a bamboo-basket (1) lined with *shibu-gami* (tough red waterproof paper made in Japan). He untied the cord that secured the lid, and, raising the latter, showed that the basket was full of *saké*.

"I never heard of storing wine in that fashion," said the Professor. "I wonder it does not leak out."

"It is like a stone jar," said Oto. "The paper is thoroughly waterproof."

The Samelenko showed them a bottle (3) made of the same material as the basket, and a wooden tray (4) manufactured by the Colletské, from a curious streaked wood found in the swamps of Northern Karafuto.

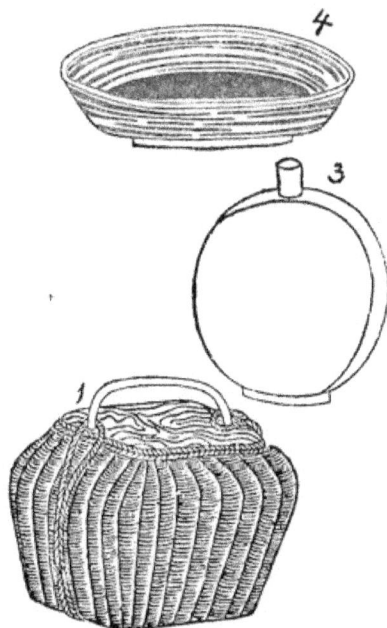

Their host very generously offered them some of the wine, and, upon their declining it, remarked, —

"Then I will drink a little in honor of the god;" adding, "I hope you will have a safe journey back."

"That is a hint for us to go," said Fitz. "There is not much to see in these places."

The old man closed his storehouse, and saluted them by bowing and repeatedly stroking his beard. When they offered him some money he shook his head, and said he did not want such a thing: it never brought him any luck; a whaling-captain once gave him a large piece of copper money for a boat-load of dried salmon, and, all the while he retained the coin, he had suffered from rheumatism.

This was translated to Fitz, who roared with laughter, and said, —

"These are true savages. Now I know why the sea-captains in Cromlech used to collect the big old copper pennies. They brought them out here, and invested them in dried fish."

Mrs. Jewett and Sallie felt tired, so retired to the tent, leaving the gentlemen to take a stroll in the country.

"We have a convict-establishment about a mile from here," said the lieutenant. "Would you like to walk over and inspect it?"

"No: I dislike to witness human misery," answered the gentleman. "No doubt the prisoners have broken your laws, or committed some crime that calls for their punishment; but I do not desire to see them."

"Oh!" cried Fitz. "What is that under the tree? A bow and arrow with a fish tied to it."

"It is a Samelenko otter-trap," said the Russian. "Do not

go near it: the barb is poisoned. When the otter seizes the fish, it pulls the trigger, and the arrow transfixes the poor brute."

"Well, what with otter, fox, and bear traps," said Johnnie.

SAMELENKO OTTER-TRAP.

"I do not think walking in Karafuto is very healthy exercise. Come, suppose we return to mother and Sallie."

The travellers camped out that night, and did not wake until late the next morning, when they embarked for Ishirao.

CHAPTER XII.

MOVING UP THE WESTERN COAST OF KARAFUTO.

" If you would cross a rapid stream, do not attempt to row straight over. You must go with, and not against, the water-god." — SAMELENKO SAYING.

THE man-of-war was nearly all day steaming from Hokobi to Ishirao.

" Why are we thus delayed ? " inquired Sallie.

" The current is very strong in this part of the strait, and our boilers are somewhat shaky," replied Capt. Imadate. " I shall have to hug the shore very closely, or we might come to grief. I've had some narrow escapes in these waters, the shifting sands being exceedingly treacherous."

As the vessel approached Ishirao, they saw the rocks cropping up, like teeth, right across the channel.

" I shall anchor presently," remarked the captain : " we could not get round this point to-night, it being now dead low tide. Do you notice the Russian flag on the bluff to our right ? "

" Yes," answered the Professor : " they appear to be making good use of their acquisition. I find they have military stations on all these headlands."

" Those are for the coast-guards, who keep a sharp lookout for runaway convicts," said Lieut. Koski, who just then came on deck. " Some of the rascals are always trying to escape, and we have to prevent them from crossing to the mainland."

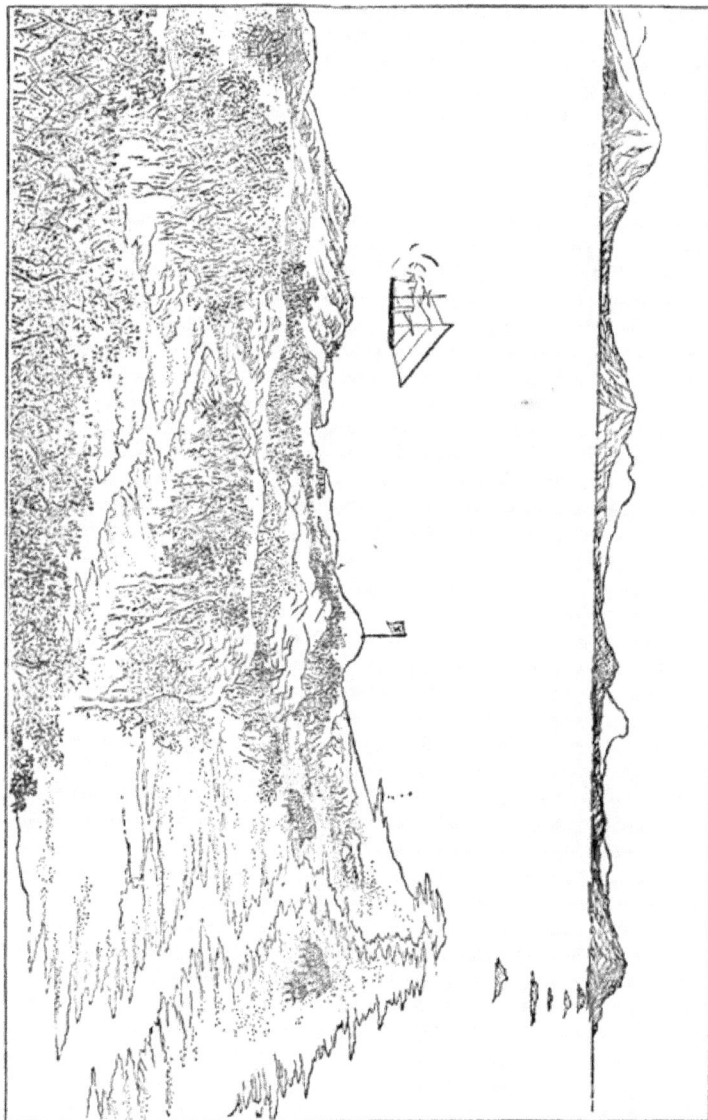

ISHIBAO. COAST OF TARTARY IN DISTANCE.

" What place is that, opposite us?" asked Fitz.

" That is Buiro, in Eastern Tartary," was the reply.   " It is
ten miles from here; but, the current being exceedingly swift,
the Samelenko, who embark from this place, generally land at
an island called Waruke, that lies off Hokobi, or a little lower
down, at Washifune, which is the nearest point between this
island and the mainland."

BOYS FISHING.

The next morning the ladies decided to go on shore with
the gentlemen : so the party embarked in the captain's gig, and
were rowed up a little creek, in the mouth of which two boys
were fishing.

One of them, who was in a small canoe, wore his hair like
an Aino, and was busily engaged driving the fish by agitating
the water with two sticks.   The other held the end of the net
across the mouth of the creek, and jerked it in a peculiar

manner, in order to keep the floats on the surface of the water.

"That boy in the boat is of the Colletské tribe," said the lieutenant. "They look like the Ainos, but are very much more intelligent."

The lads raised their net, which was half full of fish, and,

SAMELENKO UNDERGROUND DWELLING.

dragging it on shore, proceeded to string its contents upon long rushes, which they suspended from the neighboring bushes.

"The Samelenko of this place live in underground houses," said their guide; "the remarkable thing being the stone foundations of the structures, and the absence of the usual fireplace in the centre of the room."

The party entered one of the dwellings, which, though it smelled like a smoke-house, was tidily kept.

"Their carpenter-work pleases me," said Sallie. "Do you notice how nicely that double table is made? They have iron axes and knives, porcelain bottles and jars, and a little fireplace with a pan over it, the same as you see in Japan."

In one house they found a woman amusing her baby, who, lashed in his cradle, was suspended from a curious apparatus hung from the roof. His mother was talking to him, and he was laughing as though he enjoyed what she said.

"How long do they keep their children buttoned up in those contrivances?" inquired Fitz.

"Until they are four years old," answered the lieutenant.

"What!" cried the boy, "do you mean to tell me that they are thus restrained until they are that age? You would not keep an American baby in such a machine for ten minutes. How do they learn to walk?"

SAMELENKO BABY.

"That child is now practising," replied the Russian. "He cannot go very far, and his mother always knows where he is. They seldom cry, and are very sweet-tempered and gentle."

"Well, that sort of board and lodging would break a young American citizen all up," said the boy, critically regarding the little Samelenko, who was shuffling about on an oval piece of wood placed beneath its feet. "They once put me in a baby-jumper; but I broke the cord, and got away."

"O mother! isn't this baby cunning?" said Sallie to her parent, who just then entered. "Please, Lieut. Koski, ask the woman if I may take him out of his cradle."

"Off his plank, you mean," said Johnnie. "I think this is one of the most comical sights we have seen since we left home."

The woman said the child would feel uncomfortable if she unfastened him before night-time, and begged they would excuse her from doing so.

"Give him some candy, sis," said Fitz: "he will like that."

The young lady felt in her pockets, and presently brought out a bag containing peppermint-lozenges, one of which she put in the child's mouth.

The little fellow continued to smile for a few seconds, then spat out the candy, and set up a dismal howl.

"What is the matter?" inquired Mrs. Jewett.

"It set my mouth on fire!" cried the youngster, as the tears streamed from his eyes. "I'm burning."

His mother gazed on him with alarm, then caught him, cradle and all, to her bosom, and, after kissing the terrified one, said,—

"Oh, my poor child! what have they done to you?"

In a few moments he ceased his noise, and began to lick his lips, then hunted round for the rejected lozenge.

"I guess he is all right now," said Johnnie. "It scared him at first, but I thought he would be converted after the first taste."

The mother examined the candy, and tasted it, after which

she passed it to her husband, who smelt it suspiciously, and said, —

"I believe it is dangerous! I never eat any thing that I am not sure about."

When this was translated, Fitz said to his father, —

"He is a wise man. Don't you think so, sir?"

The Professor shook his finger at him, and replied, —

"I do not wish to be reminded of my imprudence."

"I did not mean the stew, sir," said the irrepressible.

Mrs. Jewett, who was laughing at them, said, —

"Here comes Capt. Imadate. I suppose it is time for us to go on board again."

"You are quite right, madam," answered the commander. "The tide is favorable for passing through the shoals, and I want to reach Tamurao before dusk. It does not do to make a port on this coast after dark."

When they reached the beach, they found the tide coming in furiously between the sand-banks.

"There are our young friends, the Samelenko and Colletské fishermen," said Johnnie. "What are they doing with that rope?"

At that moment a boy came rushing along the opposite sand-spit, shouting, and waving his hands, in order to drive a flock of snipe that flew before him. As the birds approached the boys with the rope, they half closed their eyes, then suddenly whirled the cord, and knocked two of the snipe into the water.

"Well, that beats every thing," cried Fitz. "I have heard of catching trout with a hammer, but never before knew any one who went sniping with a rope."

They watched the lads catch a number of birds, then the

party embarked on board the man-of-war. As they steamed along the shore, they noticed the strait was wider.

" We shall soon lose sight of Tartary," said the commander. " At Tamurao one can only see some islands that lie off the opposite coast, and a faint outline of the distant mountains."

It was quite dark when they entered Tamurao Harbor, — a sort of channel worn between two points of low land, on the

NOVEL METHOD OF CATCHING SNIPE.

extreme ends of which lights were hoisted for the guidance of the man-of-war.

It being too late to land, the travellers passed the evening in writing and reading.

Early the next morning Lieut. Koski summoned the boys, saying, —

" There is going to be a funeral on shore : would you like to witness it ? "

"Certainly," answered Fitz. "Can Sallie go too? She always likes to attend all such affairs."

"I think she might," was the reply, "though you will not witness a very impressive ceremony."

Breakfast was hastily served; and the party landed, but they could not discover any signs of a village.

"The settlement is about a mile off," said the lieutenant. "I suppose you do not mind walking."

PORT TAMURAO.

"I reckon we will have to, as I do not see any hacks round," said Fitz. "I think that the family ought to have sent us conveyances."

The Professor frowned; and Fitz, taking the hint, ceased making fun.

The road lay through a wooded district, swarming with mosquitoes and flies, which, as usual, settled in clouds upon the foreigners' garments.

"There will be another funeral before we get through

with this expedition," said Fitz. "There won't be much of my remains to bury: these horse-stingers are carrying me off piecemeal."

Oto, who was of a very inventive turn, made fly-flappers of some long, silky grass, and presented them to the ladies.

"I never thought of that," said Fitz, as he cut some of the grass for himself. "Oto, you shall have a medal. Now we can get even with these pests."

Tamurao was a miserable affair, consisting of a few straggling huts, and the cemetery, a small enclosure behind the chief's residence, in which also stood a shed containing his provisions.

"I do not see the grave," remarked Johnnie.

Lieut. Koski pointed

SAMELENKO TOMB.

to a little hut (A) built of pine-boards, that had been recently erected near the storehouse (B), and said, —

"The woman was interred under that structure."

"Was?" queried Johnnie. "I thought we were coming to a funeral."

"These Samelenko bury their dead before they hold the funeral-service," replied the lieutenant; "that is, they bury the women, but put the men up in the mountains."

"Your statement is most interesting," said the Professor. "These tribes seem to be very much like our Indians."

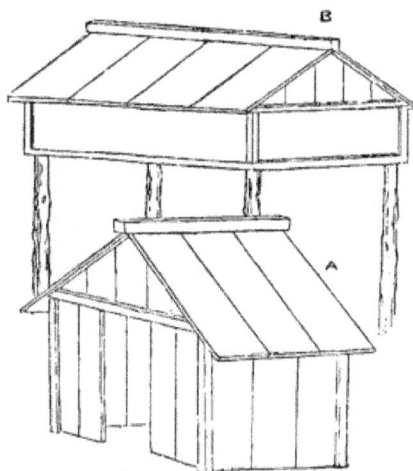

Just then a man, carrying two wooden trestles and a lot of
evergreens, came in sight, and, after gaping at the visitors,
deposited his burden near the door of the hut. As he did so,
he uttered a peculiar sound, something like the Aino cry, and
clapped his hands nine times.

"I guess that is the signal: the perform — I mean ceremony — is going to begin," said Fitz.

In a short time a procession appeared, bringing a slab of
white wood, pointed on the top, and a board, on which was a

FUNERAL DECORATIONS.

tray containing a dried salmon and two leaves of to-
bacco.

There was no priest;
the chief attending to the
spiritual as well as tem-
poral wants of his people,
and acting as master of
the ceremonies.

He invited the travel-
lers to seat themselves
where they could see the interior of the little hut; then, taking a
rude spade, entered the structure, and began to dig a hole.
When this was about a foot and a half deep, he directed his
people to bring in the slab, which he set upright exactly in the
centre of the building. After it was fixed to his satisfaction,
he tied six strips of a bark cloth, called *mose*, round it, laid the
board in front of it, and placed the offerings, as shown in the
picture.

While he was doing this, his assistants had erected the
trestles on each side of the door, and decorated them with
the greenery.

As soon as they had finished, all the tribe bowed, and remained with their faces to the ground for several moments, then rose, and hastily quitted the place.

"The ceremony is over," said Lieut. Koski.

"What!" said Fitz. "No prayers, no flowers, nothing but that old green stuff! These Samelenko don't know how to conduct a funeral."

The houses in Tamu-rao were differently con-structed from what the travellers had seen in other parts of the island, being built like Western log cabins, and roofed with sheets of bark kept in position by heavy limbs of trees.

The lieutenant informed them that the edifices were erected by the Colletské, who, although nomads, were the most ingenious of the five tribes.

"To-morrow we shall

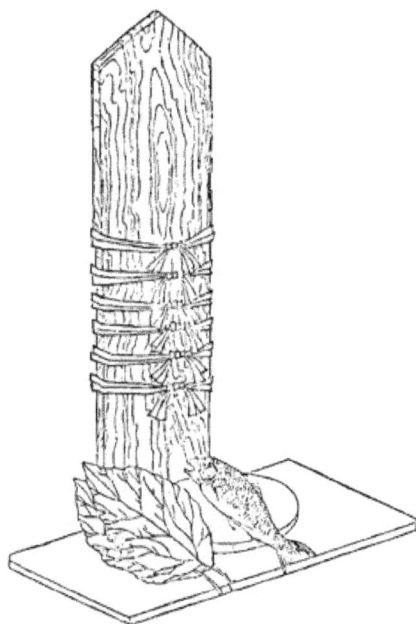

SAMELENKO WOMAN'S MONUMENT.

start for Tonu," he said. "There you will see the Colletské : they are indeed smart, and can turn their hands to almost any thing."

It did not take long to thoroughly inspect Tamurao; the only object of interest shown them being a *betch* (coat-of-mail) belonging to the chief, who said it was made by the Colletské. It consisted of a leathern coat (1) covered with plates of iron about six inches in length, and a helmet (2) of the same material.

The man appeared to be very proud of the *betch*, and assured his visitors that it would protect him against any weapon. In order to prove his assertion, he hung it on a fence, and invited his people to discharge their arrows at it.

"There!" he exclaimed, as the last shaft glanced harmlessly off. "Is not that a wonderful thing?"

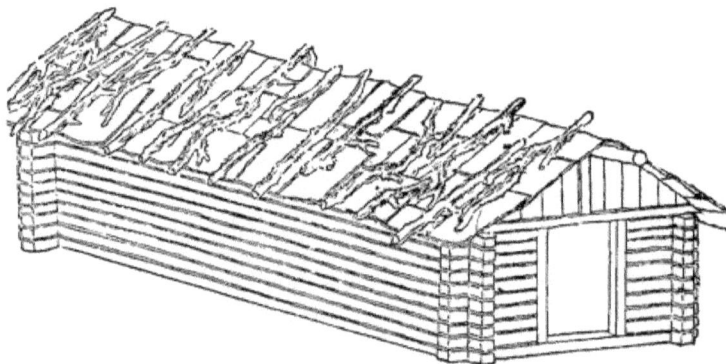

HOUSE IN TAMURAO.

"Have these people ever seen fire-arms used?" asked the Professor.

"Probably not," replied their guide. "Although they live close to the sea, they seldom go near it; and until lately, when a foreign ship approached, they would run into the woods, and hide like frightened children."

"I would love to show them the effect of a rifle-ball on that coat," said Fitz. "May I ask the chief to let me have a shot or two, sir?"

"Not on any account," replied his father. "I suppose you think it would be great fun to do what you ask."

The boy looked very penitent, and replied, —

"I thought it would be kinder humane to let them know what a decayed stick they are trusting to, sir. They are conceited about the thing now; but, if I were to put three or four balls through it, they would wake up to the fact that they had better put their trust in Providence instead of in that *belch*. May I not have just one pop at it? My act might save many valuable Samelenko lives."

"No, sir: we will leave them in their ignorance," said his father. "They are under Russian protection, and will, I dare say, never have an occasion to wear their suits-of-mail."

As they bade the chief good-by, Fitz ruefully glanced at the garment, and murmured, —

"I think it would be real missionary labor to convince the poor fellow that his tin

COAT-OF-MAIL.

suit would not stand fire. He will go on bragging about it until some drunken sailor opens his eyes with a revolver. Well, I suppose father knows best."

About four o'clock the party returned to the shore, and, re-embarking on board the man-of-war, started for the Colletské village of Tonu, on the extreme north-west point of Karafuto.

The water being very deep along the shore, the vessel kept quite close to the land, and the travellers saw some interesting sights.

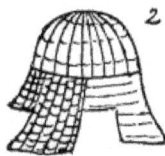

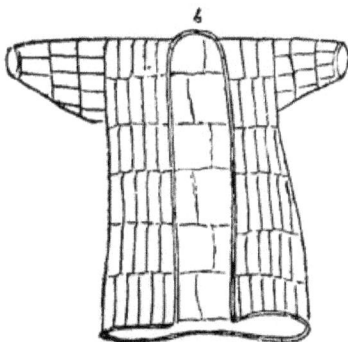

" There is a Colletské canoe," said the lieutenant, pointing to a craft drawn up on the beach. " It is made of hard wood, and is much stronger than the boats used by the other tribes."

" Look at those people leading a deer," cried Sallie, who was scanning the shore with her glass. " Both of them are armed with bows and arrows, and the woman has a quiver on her back."

" These natives sometimes train the deer to draw sleds," said their guide. " However, they usually employ dogs."

" The man is laughing, is he not? and appears to be making fun of the woman," remarked Johnnie, who was also regarding

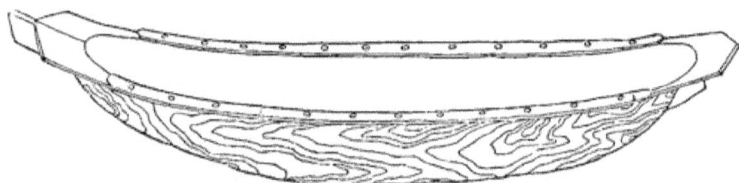

COLLETSKÉ CANOE.

the group through his glass. " Do you observe, his hair is combed back after the style of the Karafuto Ainos, and that he and the woman wear earrings like the people at Hakotan?"

" These Colletské make or import those ornaments for the Ainos," said the Russian. " They and the Santan move all over the island, and, as soon as the strait is frozen over, cross to Tartary, where they engage in trade, and work at various handicrafts."

" Look at those dogs tracking that canoe," said Fitz. " See, the man is staring at us, and not attending to his steering. They have nearly drawn his craft on shore."

The Colletské seized the hide-rope to which his animals were hitched, and jerked it over one of the bone thole-pins, on

the starboard side of the craft. This brought the latter parallel with the shore, and caused the dogs to continue their proper course.

The boilers of the man-of-war being out of order, the vessel could only steam about seven knots an hour, which rate of speed was not beyond the power of the animals.

"We are going to have a race," cried Fitz. "Isn't this fun? Modern science against five yaller dawgs."

The Colletské evidently believed that he could keep pace with the vessel, and was on his mettle. He flourished his paddle, yelled, and waved his arms in a most comical fashion, urging the willing creatures at the top of their speed.

"This is really exciting," said Sallie. "I hope the man will win: he isn't afraid to try what he can do."

"Go it, old gentleman!" cried the usually sedate Johnnie, watching their opponent through a glass. "You are game."

After racing for about a mile, during which the dogs had to swim several streams that intersected their course, the man suddenly checked them, and ran the bow of his craft on shore.

"Ah! he has given up the contest," said Mrs. Jewett.

"Not a bit of it, mamma," cried Sallie, clapping her hands gleefully. "He is real smart. He is going to land his load."

The Colletské did not take long to disembark his cargo, which consisted of a bale of dried salmon, covered with deer-skin. In another instant he was in the stern of his canoe, urging his dogs, and shouting defiantly at the man-of-war.

"Bravo, Colletské!" exclaimed the Professor. "You have true grit."

The dogs soon drew the craft ahead, and were vanishing round the base of a promontory, when the tow-line parted, and the man went backward, heels over head, into the water.

TRACKING ALONG THE SHORE WITH DOGS.

"He'll be drowned! he'll he drowned!" said Sallie, as the fellow floundered about. "I'm so sorry!"

Every one felt greatly interested, even the Japanese sailors watching the native, and commenting upon his pluck. In a few seconds he stood upright, and began to wade after his canoe, and to shout, —

"*Yek, yek!*" ("Stop, stop!")

By that time the man-of-war had gone ahead: however, nothing daunted, he secured his craft, which had drifted close in shore, whistled his animals to him, spliced his tow-line, and, once more embarking, urged them in the most frantic manner.

"Good, good!" cried the Americans.

"*Yoi, yoi!*" ("First-rate!") shouted the Japanese.

"I think I must order the chief engineer to increase our speed," said Capt. Imadate, glancing slyly at Sallie. "It will never do to allow that savage to beat us."

"Or for us to burst the boilers," was the quick response. "Oh, I hope the Colletské will win!"

As she spoke, the canoe passed the vessel; seeing which, the commander asked Lieut. Koski to hail the native, and tell him to come on board, and receive a present.

The man, instead of accepting the invitation, kept right on, and in half an hour vanished round the point of Tonu.

"I am glad he has beaten us," said Sallie. "I don't care! people who are persevering and plucky ought to win."

"You are right, Miss Jewett," said the captain. "Now we are approaching shoal-water, and will have to run farther out from the shore, or get aground."

When they were entering the harbor of Tonu, they saw the Colletské coming back at full speed.

"Why does he return?" inquired Johnnie.

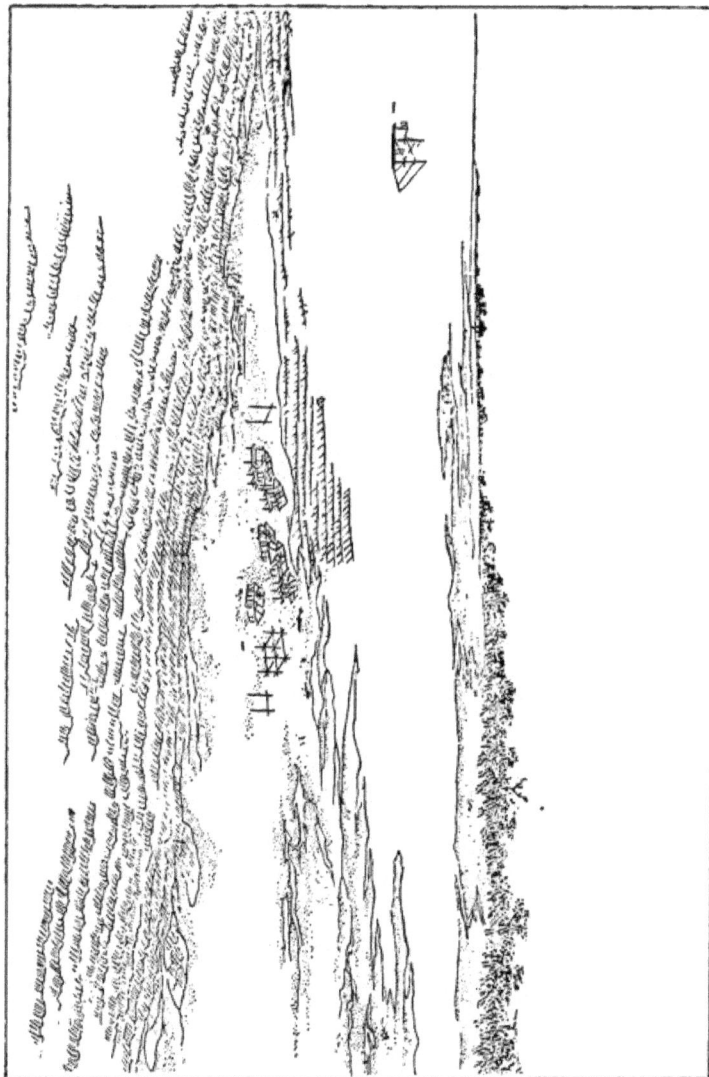

HARBOR OF TONU.

" He is going to look after his cargo," said Fitz. " He is a
deal too smart to leave it lying round loose on the shore."

About eight o'clock that evening they came to anchor in
the harbor of Tonu.

" Where is the city?" said Fitz.

" On the point to the right," replied Oto.

" You call those five huts built on piles and those fish-
flakes a city, do you?" said the boy.   " Well, I want to know!"

Oto smiled, then quietly replied, —

" Do not get excited, Fitz. Out on the plains, I have heard
two shanties and a hog-pen just as incorrectly designated."

" That's so," drawled Johnnie.   " Brother, as usual Oto has
got the best of you."

" Not a bit of it," was the sharp retort.   " If, out West,
they ever call such a small place a city, you will find a mayor
living in one of the log huts, and the aldermen in the other;
and, if a settlement is not much at first, it soon develops its
resources, — which is more than you can say of Tonu."

Then Fitz, having vindicated the national reputation, walked
forward whistling " America."

CHAPTER XIII.

WITH THE COLLETSKÉ.

" The traveller who imagines he is the first to penetrate a strange land, sees not the imprints of the billion footsteps that time has levelled in his path."

THIS Tonu is quite a place," said Fitz, who had been to the mast-head, and reconnoitred the village through a field-glass. "What time shall we go on shore, sir?"

"About nine o'clock," said his father. "I am very anxious to see the habitations of the Colletské."

HOUSE IN TONU.

The party embarked in the captain's gig, and were rowed up a creek to the town, which contained about thirty houses, built like the Samelenkos' huts, with the crevices of the beams calked with moss, and the outer and inner walls coated with a very hard plaster.

"Of what is this cement made?" asked Johnnie.

"They burn shells, and mix the lime thus procured with a clay found in the mountains," said Lieut. Koski. "It bears the heat very well; but the hard frosts cause it to crack, and come to pieces."

"Well, their architecture is an improvement on that of the Ainos," remarked Johnnie. "I suppose they took the idea of paper windows from Japan."

"No: they got that and the material from China," answered the Russian. "You would be astonished at the amount of traffic between this island and the mainland. Some of the Colletské have been to Pekin. I do not think they owe any of their civilization to Japan."

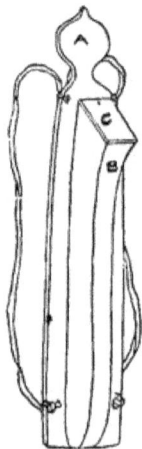

Upon entering the house, the travellers found the usual raised benches covered with mats, and noticed that the place was heated by a flue, in the Russian fashion, the smoke escaping through holes in the gables.

A woman, who was making a quiver, rose upon seeing the visitors, and exhibited her work. It consisted of two pieces, — a board (A) to

COLLETSKÉ QUIVER.

which were fastened the leathern thongs that secured it to the hunter's back; and the arrow-holder (B), which was of willow, fitted with a lid (C) of the same material.

The only instrument she used was a clumsy knife of very common iron, that required sharpening every few minutes.

She showed them a number of articles that she had made during the winter; then invited the party outside to be introduced to her husband, who was a blacksmith, and, for a savage, very wealthy.

They found him squatted behind a stone anvil, making

sickles for cutting grass. On his right was a primitive forge, the bellows of which were respectively of seal and fish skin, furnished with wooden nozzles.

As the party entered, the smith rose, and saluted them by raising his hands to the top of his head, and bringing them gradually down his face. He looked very much like a Kara-futo Aino, and had a decided cast in one of his eyes.

KOJE, THE SMITH.

"This fellow is a real good workman," said the lieutenant. "He has often been employed by our officials to rivet chains on convicts."

"Oh! you chain them up, do you?" said Fitz.

"When they are rebellious," was the quiet response. "If they do not give trouble they are allowed many privileges. — Come, Koje," to the smith, "show these visitors how you make your bellows."

Koje took, from the beams overhead, a bag made from the skin of a seal (1), one end of which was open, and the other tightly lashed around a wooden tube (2) about two feet long.

"This one is being cured," he said. "As soon as it is ready for use, I put a whalebone hoop inside it, and take a hollow piece of wood (A) in which there is a valve, gather the open end of the bag (B) together, and tie it to the handle. Two of these make one set of bellows: they last nearly a year."

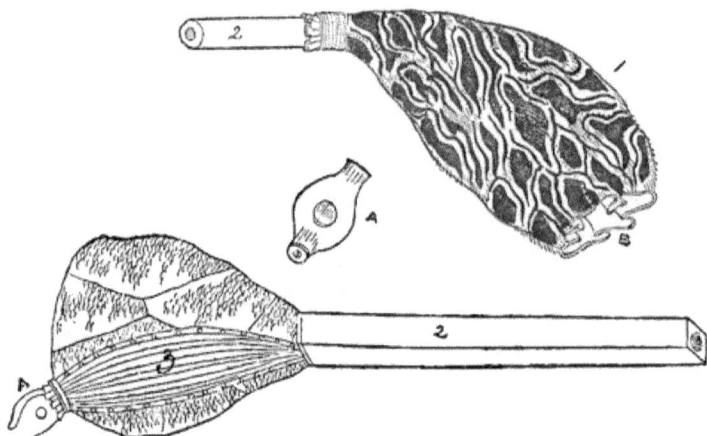

COLLETSKÉ BELLOWS.

"I see those he uses are furnished with square tubes," said Fitz, "and that one of them is made of fish-skin."

"Yes," replied the man, when the question was translated to him, "I use those because one of my sealskin bellows is worn out;" taking up the object referred to, and reversing it. "You notice, I have had to rivet a piece of deer-hide on the under side of this because the fish-skin wears out so quickly."

"Ask him to continue his work," said the Professor.

Koje complied, and, returning to his anvil, seized his

pincers, and thrust a strip of iron into the fire. One of his assistants, seated on a box, took the bellows upon his knees; while another man placed the nozzles in position, and laid a rock upon them. The bellows-blower then worked the instruments up and down, and produced a steady blast that soon brought the charcoal to a red heat.

" I see," said Johnnie. " By alternately raising the right and left bellows, he is enabled to produce a regular blast. If he worked them simultaneously, the air would only come in puffs."

" Our ancestors used the same kind of apparatus," said the Professor.

" These were copied from the Chinese," remarked the Russian.

" Japanese smiths use bellows that are very much like these," said Oto; adding quietly, "we have also adopted the American forge."

Koje gave directions to his second man, who was sharpening blades on a whetstone which he kept moist by dipping his hands in water; then the smith took up a little hammer, removed the strip of iron from the fire, and continued his labor.

" How many hours does it take him to make one of those sickles?" inquired Johnnie.

" About six," was the reply.

" How much is he paid for them?"

When this was translated, Koje scratched his ear, as though he were puzzled, and answered, —

" Sometimes I get a measure of *saké;* at others, a little rice, or a skin of millet or grain. Many people give me a skin of fish-oil, or a piece of fur to help make a garment."

" Don't they have any circulating medium here?" demanded Fitz.

"No," answered their guide: "these folks have no use for money. They supply the hunters and fishermen, and in return are furnished with food, furs, and materials for clothing. I believe there is a sort of value placed on bear, fox, otter, deer, and dog skins, that is thoroughly understood by the natives, and works very well."

"But what do they do when they go over to Tartary?" asked Johnnie.

"These Colletské understand business," answered the officer. "They will load up a sled with skins, and exchange the latter for iron, rice, *samshoo*, and whatever their trade calls for "

"What is *samshoo*?" inquired Fitz.

"Chinese *saké*," said their friend. "As you may imagine, they do not require a very elaborate system of book-keeping."

"Now I know why 'Exchange or Barter' is put in our school-books," said Fitz. "I suppose the captains of whalers who come here trade off their investments with these innocents, and the rules are put in our books for the skipper's benefit."

"We do considerable swapping in New England," said Johnnie.

"All primitive people use that method," remarked Oto.

"You don't call Massachusetts folks primitive, do you?" demanded Fitz, whose eyes flashed with indignation.

Oto gave one of his peculiar laughs, and replied, —

"Do you remember our tramp round Cape Cod? We encountered some characters almost as original as these Colletské, did we not?"

Fitz chuckled at this, and drawled, —

"Well — yeeas — so we did;" adding with a wink, "but

they all knew the value of currency. You did not find one of them refuse a dollar."

"No, nor a cent," said thoughtful Johnnie. "Oto is correct: some of our folks are — slightly primitive."

After watching the smith for a while, they bade him adieu, and went with his wife to see a man who made sleighs, snow-shoes, and boats. They found him busily engaged putting the finishing touches to a canoe (A) made of willow planks lashed together with thongs of deer-hide.

The boys examined it very attentively, then Johnnie said, —

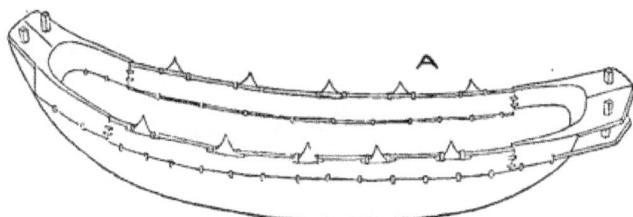

COLLETSKÉ BOAT.

"The craft we saw down the coast had the thole-pins pegged on to the gunwale, and this has them lashed. It also lacks the shoe-piece under the bow. This is poor, soft wood to make a canoe of, and it is wonderful how neatly the parts are put together. Fitz, do you see that it is calked with moss and seal-fat?"

"I do not want to see it in order to make that discovery," answered the boy. "My nose has already informed me of the fact."

"What value does he put on this?" inquired the Professor.

"I suppose," said Fitz, answering for the interpreter, "he would take a tub of *saké*, a couple of bear-skins, and a pass for the circus."

" Do be serious, sir," said his father. " My questions are
put in order to ascertain the value of certain natural and
mechanical products, and are not intended to create amusement."

" Sorry, sir," murmured the boy, moving towards a sleigh
(B) that stood under a shed near the boat. " If you want to
invest, buy this : then we could all go coasting when we get
home next winter."

The conveyance was made of a tough, light wood, the
handles being formed of whalebone, and the top of slats lashed

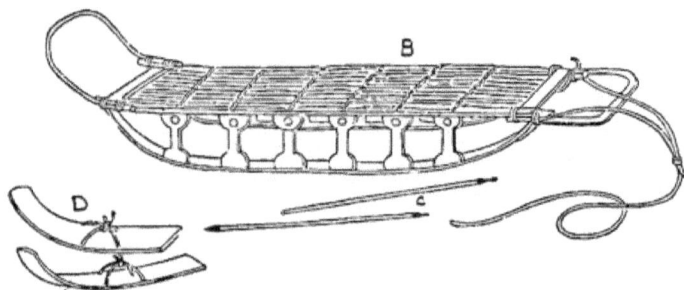

COLLETSKÉ SLEIGH.

on with deer-sinews.   It was very well constructed, and would
carry quite a load.

" These Colletské move all over the country during the
winter," said the Russian. " They harness from four to ten
dogs to these sleds, and sometimes travel sixty miles a day.
After the snow begins to fly, they never think of walking. Do
you observe that every exposed part of this vehicle is bound
with hide, and the runners are shod with bone? I have known
one of these vehicles to be loaded with two thousand pounds
of fish, after which the owner perched himself on the top of
the pile."

"What are these curled-up shingles (D) for?" asked Sallie.

"Those are snow-shoes," was the answer. "They secure them to their feet with two thongs of deer-hide, tied crosswise, and can slip them off and on like a Japanese clog."

"Are these iron-pointed sticks darts?" asked Johnnie, taking up a light staff about three feet long, the point of which was tipped with copper.

"They are used to steer the sleighs with," was the answer. "Sometimes, when the dogs are unmanageable, they are prodded with a stick."

"How cruel of them!" said Sallie.

"It does not hurt the dogs, miss," answered the amused Russian. "We use hundreds of the animals in our coal-mines. By the way, there is quite a large mine four or five miles up the creek. Would you like to visit it? The shaft is very deep, and the coal of a curious kind, containing the remains of gigantic ferns, mosses, and the trunks of trees."

"We have similar coal in our country," said Johnnie. "Do the Colletské work your mines?"

"We employ our convicts to do that," answered the lieutenant. "In the winter many of them remain under ground for several weeks at a time."

"I suppose they prefer that to running the risk of being frozen to death above," observed Fitz. "It seems very sad to exile people to such a place as this."

"They bring the punishment upon themselves," quietly returned the Russian. "Instead of working like honest men, they endeavor to live upon the weakness of their fellow-creatures, whom they make discontented and unhappy. When we catch such fellows, we send them here, and make use of them. Supposing you had a lazy, discontented, savage, unruly, ignorant class in New York, what would you do with them?"

Fitz made a comical grimace, then said, —

"Well, we would let them run our political machine. It would be better than keeping them in prison: such creatures have to live anyhow."

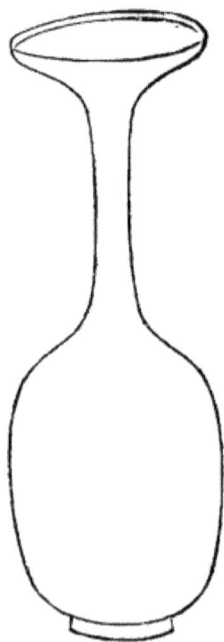

Before the travellers left, the sleigh-maker brought out a curious bottle made of metal, and a wooden cup decorated with five dots arranged in a peculiar manner.

Their host smiled, then bowed, and said, —

"Will you drink?"

"What is it?" asked Fitz.

"*Vodké*" (Russian whiskey), returned the old fellow.

"Lieut. Koski," said the Professor, "kindly explain to this gentleman, that my family has been raised upon strict temperance principles. Will you also ask him to be good enough to let me examine that bottle?"

TIN BOTTLE.

Their host did so; and, upon looking closely at the metal, he remarked, —

"Why, this is made of pure tin. Is it a product of this island?"

"No: it comes from Tartary, Professor. There are many such articles made there by the natives. You will everywhere find evidences of the close communication of the people of this island and the Tartars."

" Yes," said Oto, "that is the reason why Japan felt no compunction about ceding Karafuto to your country. We had never regarded either the Samelenko, the Colletské, the Santan, or Oroko as Japanese. Some foreigners have spoken disparagingly about our yielding part of our empire; while really, for many years, we only controlled the inhabitants of this place who lived below the forty-eighth parallel."

When the sled-maker found that his guests would not partake of his hospitality, he offered them the wooden cup which he said he had manufactured.

" Dear me!" said the Professor, regarding it with interest. " I wonder how he made this."

" Jacked it out with a knife," glibly suggested Fitz. " I do not believe there is a turning-lathe in the reservation."

" This decoration is peculiar," said his father, smilingly regarding his host. ' No doubt these five dots have a significance. Can you, Lieut. Koski, ascertain what it is?"

While their friend was endeavoring to extract the information from their host, Fitz whispered to his father, —

" I know, sir. It is intended to represent a man's eyes, nose, and mouth. Art is in its infancy up in these regions. They do not understand any thing about tone and color-harmony."

" Your son guessed rightly," said the Russian. " Those dots were intended to represent a friend of this man's who died last winter."

" He must have been very homely-featured," said Fitz. " Hullo! what is the old fellow going to show us now?"

The man went to his storehouse, and brought out a straight sword (1), and a bow (2) and arrow (3), which he offered to the Jewett boys, saying, —

" I am a very humble person, and not wealthy: still, having honored me with your presence, I cannot let you go away empty-handed. Please accept this sword: it was forged by my brother, who was swallowed by a whale several years ago."

" He must have been a Colletské Jonah," said Fitz.

" He means that his brother was killed by a whale," quietly answered the lieutenant. " He says that bow is made of a tough wood, found only near this place."

" Were they manufactured by his brother Jonah?" said Johnnie, who was sceptical about the story.

" No: they are of his own make, and the arrow is poisoned," was the reply.

"Come," said the captain, looking in at the door. " We are going to have some rough weather, and I am anxious to get round to Toronto on the north-east side. It has a fine harbor, and if a hurricane comes on we can ride it out there."

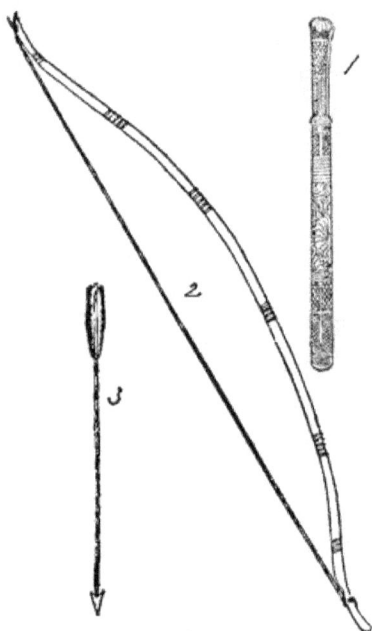

COLLETSKÉ WEAPONS.

The travellers bade adieu to Tonu, and, embarking on board the ship, steamed round the extreme northern point of Kara-futo, and started down the east coast.

It took them a day and a night to reach Toronto Bay; by which time the strong breeze, blowing when they started, had

TORONTO BAY.

culminated in a hurricane, that kept them on board the vessel forty-eight hours after they came to anchor.

When the gale was over, they landed, and found two Santan girls cleaning salmon upon the beach. Their hair was dressed in a mixed Aino and Tartar style; and both of them were very merry and free, saluting the travellers without the least sign of

SANTAN GIRLS.

embarrassment. They wore buttons on their dresses in Chinese fashion, and one of the girls had her robe trimmed with brass rings the size of a silver dollar.

The maidens were so busy that they did not stop while chatting with the visitors, but talked and worked, saying, —

"The gale caused the fish to retire to deep water; but, as soon as they knew that the wind was abating, they returned in great numbers, and this morning our people have had their nets full."

The Santans were living in their summer-quarters, which consisted of tents made of the skins of fishes, rudely sewn together upon a frame composed of roughly cut saplings tied with thongs of deer-hide.

The party entered one of the structures, which, though bare of furniture, was neatly kept, and waterproof.

" How light it is ! " said Fitz. " It is like a tent made of oiled paper."

" Yes, and quite as mal-odorous," said Johnnie.

" Well, you cannot expect dried fish-skin to have the

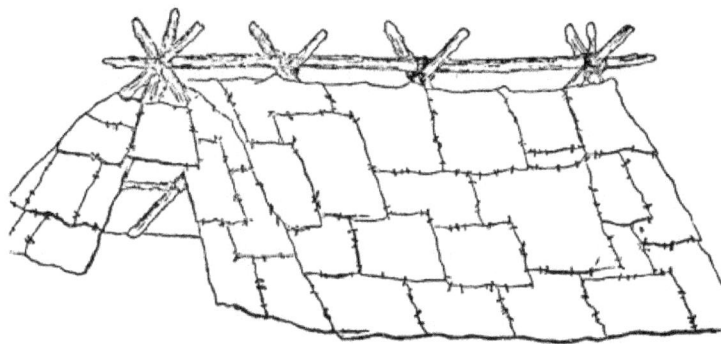

SANTAN SUMMER RESIDENCE.

delightful perfume of a rose," said Fitz as they quitted the structure. " I think this is a smart idea. The only thing is, it strikes me as being an awful waste of glue-material."

" Why do they call this place Toronto?" inquired Sallie of the lieutenant. " Did they borrow the name from Canada ? "

The Russian laughed, and replied, —

" The fact is, the Santans originated the name : so the Canadians must have appropriated it."

" For what is that heavy roof?" asked the Professor, pointing to a structure behind one of the tents.

"That is a summer storehouse. It is built and roofed with saplings in order to protect the fish from the crows, which are very great thieves. Do you have those birds in America?"

"Yes," said Fitz: "they yanked up all the pease I planted one spring."

SANTAN STOREHOUSE.

"'Yank' is not an elegant word, my son," whispered his mother.

· "I understand his meaning," said the Russian.

"It is in the dictionary," murmured the boy.

"Mamma knows that," said Sallie; "but we do not use all the words we find there."

"Oh! I suppose you have made a special study of the lexicon," retorted Fitz. "I understand, in future I shall have to weigh every word before I use it."

This difference of opinion highly amused Lieut. Koski; who

politely waited until the discussion had ended, then said to the Professor, —

" Look at those *tona kai* " (deer). " The Santans use them to draw their sleds ; are they not curious creatures ? "

The gentleman led the way to the group of animals, and after examining them said, —

" These must have been imported from Tartary. I do not think they can be indige-nous. Come, Fitz, exercise your powers of observation. Which species of deer do you consider this to be ? "

SANTAN DEER (TONA KAI).

The boy made a grimace, as though he disliked being catechised, placed his right elbow in the palm of his left hand, and rested his chin upon his right (his father's favorite position when lec-turing), then said, —

" The palmate lower horns, and cylindric upper, would lead me to infer these to belong to the *Kangifer-carabou;* but, from the extraordinary length of their tails, I should imagine they are the missing link between the mule and the deer. I should conjecture that the extreme length of their caudal appendages has been caused by the continual at-tention brought to bear upon them by the Santan drivers, who, no doubt, use them as reins."

" That will do, sir," sternly answered his parent. " When I

question you with regard to your progress in the science of zoölogy, I do not desire such a flippant reply."

"Very sorry, sir," was the penitent response. "I could not resist telling you what I thought."

The travellers visited several huts, and would have staid a day or two at Toronto, but were driven on board the ship by dense clouds of smoke that came from the south, and rendered sight and breathing very difficult.

As they were embarking, the lieutenant said, —

"The ground is on fire down by Hento. In some places the soil is covered for several feet with dead leaves, that mat together; and, the summers being dry, they do not rot."

"I remember tumbling into one of those holes," said Fitz. "It was filled with dust-like peat."

"Yes," responded the Russian: "the powder resembles punk, and burns quite slowly. The natives are very careless, and, when they light a fire in the woods, are too stupid to think of extinguishing it. These slow fires will burn for months, and sometimes years, and during the summer-time are often very troublesome, suffocating numbers of the natives."

"Say," cried Fitz, as though suddenly remembering something, "what is to-day?"

"The last of September," answered his father. "How the time has flown! It will be winter by the time we arrive home."

"Home!" echoed Johnnie. "Are we really going, sir?"

"Yes," replied his father. "I have decided to decline the offer of the Japanese Government, which wishes me to remain in Japan for another term of years. Your mother has had enough of travelling; and I want you, boys, to go to college."

" 'Rah!" cried Fitz. "That is good news. I am really hungering for a sight of old Cromlech. Here we are alongside the ship. — Mother, let me help you up."

In half an hour they were steaming down the burning coast for Horonai.

CHAPTER XIV.

AMONG THE OROKO.

"When the rats come indoors, it is time to examine your winter kimono"
(clothes). — JAPANESE PROVERB.

IT is growing cold," said Sallie, as she promenaded the deck
with her father. "I should not be astonished if we had a
flurry before we get clear of Karafuto. The winter begins very
early in this region, does it not, Capt. Imadate?"

Their friend smiled, and said, —

"Yes; but even if we have a slight fall of snow, I do not
believe it will inconvenience you. Here is Lieut. Koski: he
knows more about it than I do."

The Russian smiled, and said, —

"The natives welcome the beautiful snow: it enables them
to get about, and to visit distant places. At the first fall
they harness their dogs or deer, and are off upon trading-
expeditions."

"You quoted 'Beautiful Snow,'" said Sallie. "Have you
ever heard the American poem of that name? About a hundred people claim to have written it."

"We once had a similar bone of contention in Russia," said
the lieutenant; "but the authorship was easily decided, the
emperor announcing that the writer, or whoever claimed to be
such, was to be banished to Siberia, which quickly settled the
question."

"There is Horonai right ahead," said Capt. Imadate. "We shall come to anchor about nine o'clock, and you can disembark in the morning. I think you will be very much interested in the Oroko tribe. I shall be compelled to leave you on shore for a few days while I run back to see if I can render the Santans any assistance. Lieut. Koski is afraid the loss of life through this fire will be severe. Both Hento and Chia are enveloped in a dense body of smoke, and I fear the inhabitants have not sufficient means of quitting the land."

"We do not mind tenting it," said Mrs. Jewett. "I am very glad you are going to the assistance of the poor people."

They disembarked early on the following morning, and found themselves in a land-locked harbor, which was, however, more shallow than any they had before visited. The Russian flag was flying above some houses occupied by the coast-guard; and Lieut. Koski told the travellers that about two miles in the interior there were very extensive coal and copper mines, worked by the exiles.

"What mountain is that over to the left?" asked Sallie.

"Mount Kitoshi," said their friend. "We saw it on the other side. The island is very narrow, and is a mass of volcanic formations."

The boys hoisted a Japanese and an American flag on the tent, and the sailors cut a supply of wood to last the party several days; then the captain returned on board his ship, and proceeded up the coast.

"How very cold it is growing!" said Fitz with a shiver. "I wish we had brought our overcoats."

About nine o'clock the snow began to fall, and by noon it stormed in earnest.

"This is pleasant," said Johnnie. "We cannot light a fire

HORONAI.

in here, for fear of burning down the tent. I am afraid we shall be half-frozen before the ship returns."

In a few moments Lieut. Koski, who had been out in search of the Oroko village, re-entered, and said, —

"I have got some news for you. I met the chief of this tribe, who will presently bring a sled to take you to his dwelling."

As he spoke they heard voices outside, and some dogs barking.

"Let us go and see," cried Fitz, who, enveloped in a bear-skin robe, looked very much like the animal. "Is not this fun!"

The whole party followed him, and beheld two Orokos on a sled drawn by three dogs. The men saluted by placing their fingers on their foreheads; and the chief said to the lieutenant, —

"We have only three skins of oil which we can leave here. Please ask your friends to get on the sled, and tell them I will carry them to my house. I shall be very much honored by their taking up their abode there."

The boys assisted their mother and sister upon the vehicle, then, with their father, Oto, and the lieutenant, took their places.

"All aboard!" shouted Fitz. "The next stop will be at the Horonai Hotel."

The men fastened an extra rope to the sled, and, shouting to the dogs, started at a rapid run.

In about twenty minutes they arrived at their destination, which proved to be quite a well-built structure, and was really very clean and cosey.

"This man's name is Ippu," said their guide. "He is the chief of the Oroko tribe."

OROKO TRIBE.

"I should not have known it," observed Fitz. "He does not put on any frills."

"He wants to speak to you," continued Lieut. Koski, as the party seated themselves upon the matted floor.

"Tell him we are all attention," said the Professor. "And please inform him that if he will kindly let his house, we will pay any sum he requires."

The Oroko bowed very low, then said,—

"This is a very poor place. I have nothing here, but those old swords and the lacquer tubs, worth your looking at. You are from a distant land, and need shelter : accept my home, and I will go into the reindeer-shed, which is very warm and comfortable."

While this was being translated, Fitz said in an undertone to Sallie, —

"He is like old Hardcase at Cromlech, who used to let his house, furnished, to summer boarders, and take up his abode in the hay-loft."

Sallie gave him a cautionary signal, and the Professor looked very grave, so the boy did not continue his remarks.

Ippu was about to retire, when the Professor said, —

"Please ask him to stay a moment, and request him to tell me what remuneration he expects."

When this was translated, the man said, —

"I do not understand you. I cannot sell my home ; and, as for your staying here, you will honor me greatly by doing so."

"I wonder whether one of our boarding-house keepers would consider the honor of Ippu's company sufficient pay," whispered Fitz to his sister. "He is a genuine savage. Gives up his house, and says that he does not want any thing for his trouble. Isn't he an innocent?"

Finding the chief would not agree to accept any payment, they allowed him to retire; then all hands set to work to make themselves comfortable.

They found a tub full of fresh spring-water, and a stone trough in which they made bread. There were two iron kettles hung upon the walls, from which were also suspended a copper axe, two iron frying-pans, lacquer boxes containing rice, some fine swords, quivers of arrows, fish-spears, and *inaho*.

Fitz and Johnnie climbed up a notched pole, and surveyed the contents of the attic.

Oto, Mrs. Jewett, and Sallie built a fire on the hearth in the centre of the room; and the Professor "mooned" round, and made notes of the furniture.

" How do they use these two curious pieces of wood, hanging near this stone trough?" asked the Professor.

"Those are wooden hams, sir," said Fitz. " I guess they got the pattern from some Fall-River whaler. Those indigestible counterfeits must have found a ready market among these guileless Orokos."

" Those pieces are used as clappers, in order to give an alarm in case of fire," said the lieutenant. " They do look something like hams."

Mrs. Jewett called every one to assist in preparing the meal; and they had a very merry time, the building being filled with dense smoke in which they could hardly distinguish each other.

After a while they discovered a ventilator; and by dint of opening it, and rolling up the reed blind that served as a door, they contrived to render the atmosphere bearable.

That night they slept soundly upon the matted floor, while outside the snow was falling, and the wind blowing furiously.

After breakfast the next morning, an Oroko, clad in a bear-

skin coat and cap, tiger-skin knickerbockers, and seal-skin leggings and wooden snow-shoes, stopped outside the building, and began to summon their host.

Lieut. Koski went to the door; whereupon the man raised his hand to his forehead, and said, —

"My sister has just died, and I want Ippu to come to the funeral."

"There are foreigners here with me," said the Russian. "Ippu is staying in his deer-shed."

The man again saluted, then, throwing his spear over his shoulder, went off to find his friend.

"How much the costumes of these men resemble those of the old Japanese archers!" said Professor Jewett. "I suppose both were copied from the ancient Tartar dress."

"Why does he carry a spear in his hand, and have a reed mat and some codfish upon his back?" asked Sallie.

BAD NEWS.

"He requires the weapon to defend himself against the bears," replied the Russian. "Sometimes, when the wind blows very high, these men have to camp out in the woods; when they make a tent-pole of their spear, and, covering it with a mat, crawl under it, and go to sleep. They use the dried fish as we do bread."

The storm did not abate much during the day, so the travellers contented themselves with watching the dog-sleighs pass and repass. The animals evidently knew the hut contained strangers; for they invariably stopped in front of the door, and refused to go until they had satisfied their curiosity by gazing on the new-comers.

One sled, drawn by six dogs, was delayed for over half an hour, and afforded great amusement to the young people.

The man who drove the team was a powerfully built Oroko, and so enveloped in bearskins that Fitz named him Capt. Boynton, whom he somewhat resembled. He steered the sled by a dexterous use of his snow-shoes, and a staff pointed with copper, and managed the dogs with a single hide-rope which he held in his right hand. His vehicle was laden with four skins of fish-oil, the odor of which was perceptible in the hut.

After a while the man became very angry, and abused his dogs in a shrill falsetto; whereupon they suddenly swerved to the right, threw him upon the snow, and set off homeward as hard as they could run.

The spectators laughed until the tears ran down their cheeks; for instead of rising, and following his dogs, the fellow sat up on the snow, and howled like a child.

"His is not the Aino whine," said Johnnie. "I do not believe our friends in Yezo would be guilty of such babyish behavior."

Presently the man uttered a prolonged bark, then rose, adjusted his foot-gear, and started in pursuit of his dogs.

The fall continued until about five o'clock, when the boys put on native snow-shoes, and went out to reconnoitre.

There was one underground dwelling in the village; and, as it was covered with snow, the young Americans had an

CAPT. BOYNTON.

opportunity of understanding why it was built in that peculiar manner.

"I comprehend," remarked Johnnie: "by partly sinking their dwellings, they are enabled to keep them very warm, and at the same time to obtain ventilation."

"The structures that are entirely built above ground are exceedingly cold, and are more liable to be blocked with snow, than these," said the lieutenant.

"I would not like to live up here," said Fitz. "Just imagine burrowing like bears during six months in the year. How sad it must be for the Russian exiles!"

The lieutenant smiled at this, and said, —

"They are nearly all underground during the winter: besides, they have their minds and bodies employed, and are better off than many people in Russia. As to the natives, if this snow continues, there will not be an Oroko here in a week. They will close their huts, and migrate. The winter to them is what the summer is to us."

That evening the travellers sat round the fire, and listened to Lieut. Koski's stories of Russian life; then, when the Professor announced it was past midnight, retired to their mats.

About six o'clock the next morning Fitz called out, —

"I do not know how you are, but I am unpleasantly warm."

"So am I," answered his father, who had been lying awake for some time. "Another hot wave has ascended from the south, and will soon melt the snow."

The boy went to the door, and, pulling aside the mat, glanced out, and said, —

"It has already vanished. The rain is coming down, and the ground looks like a sponge."

After the party had breakfasted, Ippu called upon them, and said, —

"Would you care to see the funeral?"

"Thank you," answered the Professor. "We should very much like to be present."

"Then, please come with me."

Lieut. Koski, who had been out watching for the arrival of the ship, said to his friends, —

"If you take my advice, you will remove your boots and stockings, and roll up your pants over your knees, then put on the native sandals. The ground is just like a pudding, and in some places is a deep bog."

Ippu told them to take the fishing-spears for poles, and, if they felt themselves sinking deeply, to call to him at once.

WOMAN'S MONUMENT.

They walked about three-quarters of a mile, then arrived at a little valley, scattered about which were some curious monuments, made of wood.

"These are the women's tombs," said their guide. "The Orokos can tell, by the decoration on the horizontal piece, the name of the person to whose memory the monument is erected."

"How can they do that when they have no alphabet?" inquired Johnnie.

" Of course the signs are arbitrary," was the reply.

" I understand," answered the lad. " It is like an old man who used to sell fish in our place. He made one wriggle for our name, and two for our neighbor's, and so on. But when he died nobody could unravel his accounts, so they adjudged him a bankrupt."

The Russian smiled at this, and remarked. —

" We have just such characters in my native place. The world is very much alike, all over."

While they were chatting, a procession approached, bearing the body of the woman.

No one displayed any very great grief, nor was there any exhibition of indifference. They moved in and out among the tombs until they reached a shallow grave, where they halted : then the chief gave the order, the body was interred without any words being spoken, and the Orokos moved quickly away, as though in a hurry to quit the spot.

" The men are never buried," said their guide. " Sometimes they are placed in a coffin, which is deposited up in a niche in the mountains ; but, as a rule, they are exposed in some out-of-the-way place, and are gradually absorbed by the elements."

" What is their marriage-ceremony like ? " said the Professor.

" It resembles that of the Ainos of Yezo," replied their friend. " There are a number of Russian *papas*" (priests) " in this island, and I suppose half of the five tribes have been baptized ; but I do not think any of the converts understand the nature of the ceremony."

" I should imagine not," said the Professor. " Although the Samelenko, Santan, Colletské, and Oroko tribes have sufficient intelligence to satisfy their bodily wants, their mental capacity is comparatively undeveloped."

"That is why my nation has such contempt for them," said Oto. "I have been studying these people very closely, and believe, with their splendid cranial development, they could be taught almost any thing. They have, for centuries, been deprived of all opportunity of acquiring what we call knowledge, spite of which they have not degenerated into brutality. Of the five tribes, I prefer the Aino; they, in my opinion, being the purer race. One of the most remarkable facts concerning them is their strong resemblance to the aborigines of Australia."

Fitz, who had listened with the utmost gravity, clapped his hands, and said, —

"Bravo! Professor Nambo, you ought to be engaged by the lecture-bureau at Cromlech. They will give you chalk and a blackboard; and you can dance about the platform, and astonish folks with your wonderful diagrams. I reckon you would make your fortune in two or three years."

Oto laughed, and the lieutenant said, —

"I do not think there is any thing more to interest us in this spot."

"That is so," laughingly responded Johnnie. "The inscriptions on the tombstones are not very amusing reading."

"Let us take a walk on the shore," suggested their father.

"It is more like wading, sir," said Fitz. "I thought the section about Ishikari Mountain was rather pulpy, but this is the land of mush."

"I wish it were a land of mush and milk," said his brother.

"I never saw such a fellow as you are to grumble, Johnnie Jewett," said Fitz.

"Well, brother, I think that remark is amusing from you," retorted Johnnie. "We have heard nothing but your growls ever since we started."

"Why, Johnnie, I only objected to getting up at uncivilized hours," was the laughing response. "I do not remember ever having complained ; do you, father?"

"I would rather not express my opinion," answered the Professor. "I am wondering how long we shall be doomed to remain in this place. Now this warm spell has come, it may be very unhealthy."

The mud was something appalling, and so greasy that the natives continued to use their sleds exactly as though the ground were still covered with snow.

When the travellers reached the shore, they found three men busily engaged loading a sled with dried fish.

"Where are they going?" inquired Fitz.

"Across the mountains to Wakee," said the lieutenant. "They can sled over this mud, and get their mats of fish on to the other side of the island, before the deep snows set in."

"What will they do with it?" asked Johnnie.

"Take it across to Tartary," was the reply. "Some of this fish finds its way into the heart of China."

"How are they paid for it?"

"In brass ornaments, scrap-iron, and the other things which these people value. Each sled will carry eight mats of fish, and a driver ; and, upon an average, the dogs will run twenty miles a day."

Fitz, who had attentively watched the men, whistled in a peculiar fashion, and whispered to his father, —

"I have made a discovery, sir. These Orokos are one of the lost tribes of Israel. Look at their noses."

The Professor shook his head reprovingly, but could not avoid smiling.

They watched the natives catch a dog, that was evidently unwilling to be harnessed to the sled, and which was dragged along to the hitching-post as a nurse drags an unruly child.

The men were some time packing the vehicle, and starting the team: however, it finally got away, and went gliding through the mud at a rapid pace.

As the party saw it disappear, one of the Oroko pointed down the bay, and said, —

"There is the ship!"

"Good news, good news!" shouted the boys; then they waded back to Ippu's hut, and communicated the intelligence to Mrs. Jewett.

An hour afterwards they were once more on board the man-of-war, and were steaming down the coast for Chika-hiroshi Bay.

CHAPTER XV.

ADIEU TO KARAFUTO.

"The discarded pottery of a nation is often the only record of its existence."

THE man-of-war touched at Wencotan, Nui, Kun, and Kukina, at which place they saw the last of the Oroko tribe. Then they steamed round the cape of Sinpu-shiritoco, and ran westward across Chika-hiroshi Bay to Horono, one of the two famous mountains of Karafuto.

As they sighted the towering peak, they noticed that only its summit was covered with snow, which made the pinnacles resemble gigantic stalagmites.

The temperature, which in latitude fifty-one had been low enough to be exceedingly unpleasant, was here quite high. This determined the travellers to remain a day or two, and see something more of the Ainos of Karafuto.

Col. Goshkoff, the Russian officer in charge of the convict establishment at Horotoki, the town at the base of the mountain, came off to the ship to welcome them. He was a very hospitable gentleman, who had once been attached to the legation at Washington, and was therefore exceedingly pleased to see any one from the States.

He begged them to stay with him, and told the Professor that a wonderful piece of old pottery had recently been discovered by some Ainos who were prospecting on the mountain side.

"You really must come on shore with me," he said. "I have a large house; and my wife, who accompanied me to America, will be delighted to entertain you. My boat is alongside, and you only have to enter it."

The Professor accepted the invitation; and the travellers were rowed on shore in a Russian launch, manned by thirty convicts.

The first sight that greeted them on landing was two Ainos, performing *ouri*. They were dressed somewhat differently from the Yezo-jin, wore skin - robes trimmed with brass ornaments, and had a wheel pattern embroidered on each shoulder, but otherwise were very much like their brethren on the next island.

KARAFUTO AINOS' OURI.

"I wonder what the decoration upon that man's robe means," said the Professor. "It is a very ancient design."

"I should think it is an advertisement for fireworks," said Fitz. "We used to see it on the papers of the crackers we burnt on the Fourth of July."

"Your son is right," said the colonel. "On the last anniversary of the emperor's birthday, I burnt some fireworks, the wrappers of which were eagerly appropriated by the Ainos, who have since used the trade-mark as a decoration for their robes."

"That only confirms my theory," said the Professor. "All the Chinese forms are of great antiquity."

They left the Ainos holding each other's hands, and weeping like children.

Mrs. Goshkoff proved to be a very charming lady; and her establishment, being kept in pure Russian style, was most interesting to the Americans.

"It is dreadful to be exiled here," she said. "I have not a soul to speak to but my husband; for one cannot associate with the prisoners, though we have many gentlemen and ladies among them."

"Why cannot you?" said Fitz. "I should think it would be better than the monotony you complain of."

"It is against the regulations," was the response. "The colonel stationed here before my husband, had charge of his own brother, who was condemned to perpetual exile. Of course, when the authorities discovered this, they recalled the officer."

"How do you amuse yourself during the long winter?" asked Sallie.

"I superintend the house, and study the customs of the Ainos," replied the lady. "I also paint a little. That," pointing to the wall, "represents Konac, our chief hunter, killing a seal on the ice. I witnessed the scene last winter."

"Why does he have a crooked spear?" asked Johnnie.

"It enables him to use it under the ice," replied the lady. "Konac is a very faithful creature, and has secured me quite a number of skins."

"He is well wrapped up, is he not?" said Fitz, adding in a musing tone, "How much do you pay him for each skin?"

"Nothing," answered the lady: "those people think it is quite enough honor if we condescend to accept their presents."

Fortunately dinner was announced, or there is no knowing

what remark Fitz might have made. He had been brought up
with sound notions about right and wrong, and did not understand the peculiar kindness that prompted a civilized lady to
accept furs from a savage ignorant of their value.

It was very amusing to hear the colonel's wife inquiring of
Mrs. Jewett and Sallie about the latest fashions in New York,

SPEARING A SEAL.

and to listen to her husband's utterances of admiration of
our freedom; similar liberal expressions of sentiment having
caused the exile of many of the prisoners under his charge.

When the travellers were retiring, he said, —

" To-morrow we will hunt a bear, reported to be near by, in
the mountains; then we can visit the native who has that
curious piece of pottery."

The party started at daybreak, and travelled in some of the

wildest scenery they had yet met with; the ladies of course
remaining at home.

"It is a little moist here," said the colonel, as they followed
the Aino guides up a cañon, through which a torrent rushed
with great impetuosity. "There are no roads, to speak of; and
when you go hunting, you have to travel like the Ainos."

ASCENDING HORONOBORI.

The mosquitoes were in clouds, and of a greater variety
than the wanderers had ever before encountered; in spite of
which no one complained, but jumped from stone to stone, and,
after a weary tramp, reached a level plateau, covered with a
very fine growth of timber. They also saw gigantic specimens
of the *bekonoshita* (mammoth dock).

"We call it *akita-buki*," said Oto; "but I never saw such
enormous ones as these in my country."

"Why is this tree barked in places?" said Fitz. "I have noticed the same thing on a trunk, a little lower down."

"That is scratched during the winter by the bears. The Ainos assert that they do it in order to know their way when the ground is covered with snow. But that is absurd: they, like all clawed animals, scratch bark or any similar substance in order to sharpen their nails."

"Yes," said Fitz with a nod. "I have seen our cat, Kitty Spot, doing the same thing."

When they arrived at the place where they expected to find the bear, they saw an old Aino hunter seated on the ground, discharging arrows at a very high tree. Every time he drew his bow, he muttered something.

"I do not see any bear up there," remarked Fitz.

"That tree is regarded as sacred," said the colonel. "Do you not notice how the top branches are studded with barbs of arrows? Sometimes the Ainos come out here in great numbers to shoot."

"A kind of target-party," suggested Fitz. "You have seen them in the States, have you not, colonel?—a lot of men in red shirts, Derby hats, mammoth gloves, and antediluvian pants, marching in bad order, under a broiling sun, with a colored boy in the rear carrying a target, and three members bearing tin-plated casters for the first, second, and third prizes."

"That is a very graphic description," said their amused host. "I have often seen them, and wondered what enjoyment there could be in their parade. This *chito-kannushi* is about the same thing."

"So the natives have a name for it, do they?" answered the boy.

"Yes," was the reply: "*chito* means shoot, and *kannushi* hit."

"Suppose they miss?" said Johnnie.

"Then they fire until they strike the tree. They will select a pine or a willow, and will discharge their arrows at it until the top is cut all to pieces. The frost generally kills it; and, if the tree survives the first winter, it becomes stunted and malformed."

"I have noticed such objects in Yezo," said Oto. "There the Ainos cover them with *inaho*. If one of their arrows hits the tree, they call themselves champion marksmen."

The Aino, who had been thus amusing himself, rose, and, after gracefully saluting the colonel, said, —

"It is sad to have to communicate bad intelligence. The bear was tired of waiting here, and has gone off to rejoin his family."

This speech afforded the Americans great amusement, the Aino having delivered it with the utmost gravity.

"I do not imagine we shall have any sport," remarked the colonel. "Would you like to call on Choko, the man who has the old piece of pottery?"

"With pleasure," said the Professor. "Much as I enjoy the chase, I greatly prefer to hunt for curios. Where was this piece found?"

"I do not know much about it," was the reply. "Some of the Ainos say, at Kushunai; and others, that it was dug up in what they call the Taiko district. The old fellow who owns it is quite a character, and will afford your boys some amusement. His hut is three-quarters of a mile from here."

The party reached the place about noon, and found Choko sunning himself outside his dwelling. He was very old, and had a natural dignity that commanded the respect of his visitors, and prevented even the mirth-loving Fitz from joking.

He saluted the new-comers gravely, and, upon being informed that they desired to see his treasure, said, —

"In the ancient times there was a woman who lived near the mountain road called Inao-karusi. She was a very able person, and understood more than any other female since the time that the gods lived on the earth. Her thoughts were very deep, and she desired to benefit the Ainos. Inao-karusi is one mile from the river Hase-bets, which place was celebrated as the residence of a god who dwelt by the side of a weeping-willow tree. The old woman, who was called Taiko, from the district in which she was born, discovered how to make earthen pots, and to burn them, so that they would hold water. After many trials she produced some beautiful specimens, most of which were seven inches wide, three and a half deep, and half an inch thick. These could be put on the fire, and were twice as serviceable as the stone vessels then in use. When she had instructed the Ainos on the eastern coast how to make the vessels, she tied a pot in a cloth, and, securing it over her shoulders, started for this place. Upon reaching the base of Horonobori she stumbled, fell, and broke her treasure all to pieces. This misfortune preyed upon her mind : she became sick, and died, leaving directions that the fragments of the pot should be buried with her."

"Why didn't she set to work, and make another one?" whispered Fitz to the colonel, who was interpreting. "It strikes me that the original inventor would not have worried over losing one specimen. She would have collected some clay, built a fire, and have made another pot before you could say 'wink.'"

Col. Goshkoff smiled, then continued his interpretation, saying, —

"Ever since she was buried, the weeping-willow has been regarded as a god, the people believing that her spirit inhabits it. In the old times we used to make *inaho;* but since the change, the *batzu*" (Greek priests) "have forbidden us to cut those things."

"That is very sensible of the priests," said Fitz. "The Ainos of Yezo waste two-thirds of their time in making *inaho*, and neglect every thing in order to whittle a stick into shavings. I think these Karafuto men are smart."

The man listened gravely, and, when this was translated to him, said, —

"Young gentleman from afar, you are right. Usually the words of children have very little weight, they being mere foolishness. Would you like to see the pot?"

On being informed that was the purpose for which the visitors had come, he retired into his hut, and presently returned carrying a lacquer box, such as his people use for holding something they highly esteem. He was as bald as an egg, his forehead was corduroyed with wrinkles, his eyes dim and half closed, and his face weazened like a monkey, while his hands were so begrimed and bony that they strongly resembled birds'-claws.

He bowed first to the colonel, and then to his foreign guests, after which he placed his treasure upon the ground, and, taking off the lid of the box, revealed an article tied up in a wadded silk bag.

"Sallie ought to be here," murmured Fitz. "He is going to show us some valuable old pottery infant, worth a small fortune."

Choko slowly undid the fastenings, then produced his treasure, which, when he had caressed and rubbed, he handed to the colonel, who, after glancing at the relic, passed it to the Professor.

"This is an archaic object," murmured that gentleman. "How hard and stone-like it is! What an exquisite color! how perfect in shape!"

"Sallie would admire to see that," said Fitz to Oto. "She is way up in art-pottery jargon. She would go crazy over that old thing. It would be too exquisitely and complete- ly precious, too supremely rare, and characteristically homely! She would tell, to a day, when it was made, and give you a representation of the old woman squinting at it af- ter she had completed its manufacture. She is an

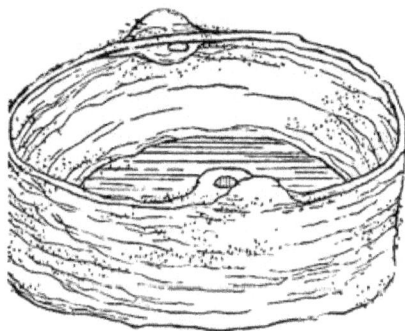

AINO "POTTERY INFANT."

expert, you know, and would term that wrinkled, corrugated, rough, common, clumsy amateur attempt at pottery-making, 'art boiled down.'"

After the Professor had regarded the specimen for several moments, he said to the colonel, —

"How these fine old pieces of pottery appeal to the culti- vated mind! I suppose that aged man would never part with such a treasure. Try and ascertain if he has any idea of its value."

The colonel and Choko argued for some time, the old gentleman evidently having made up his mind to a certain price : finally the colonel said, —

" This fellow knows too much.   He says he wants a whole tub of *saké*, and will not take less."

The Professor mused for a few moments, then replied, —

" I am, as a matter of principle, opposed to giving these people *saké*, or any thing that will increase their craving for stimulants.   However, under the circumstances, I will agree to his demand, the sacrifice being made in the cause of science."

The next day the old man came down to Horotoki, and, after delivering the piece of pottery, received his promised reward, which he, with the characteristic generosity of a savage, proceeded to share with all his tribe.

While he was still suffering from the effects of his potations, he called at the colonel's house, and, when that gentleman gave him an audience, said, —

" The generosity of these chiefs from afar is beyond my power to describe : it is as overwhelming as a rising tide. Alas! even the tide has to ebb, and I have seen the bottom of the *saké*-tub.   Will you please tell the generous stranger, if he will give me another such present, I will make him a finer piece of old pottery than the last ? "

Then the aged rogue laughed until the tears ran down his cheeks.

CHAPTER XVI.

"After a man has travelled several months, the novelty ceases to interest him, and he turns his eyes longingly towards home."
"One cannot always live on honey." — JAPANESE PROVERB.

THE party remained nearly a week at Horotoki, then, bidding adieu to Col. Goshkoff and his wife, steamed down the coast.

On the second day they touched at a place called the Fall of Huroi, an outlet of Lake Tonneicha, a large body of fresh water, situated in the highlands overlooking the ocean.

"I shall have to take my leave of you here," said Lieut. Koski. "I cannot express how much I have enjoyed your society. I hope to some day meet you again, and to renew your very delightful acquaintance."

"I am awfully sorry we are obliged to part," said Fitz. "We shall often think of you out here in the wilds. Can we not send you some papers and magazines?"

"I do not know whether they would reach me," he answered. "We seldom hold communication with Japan, and all our mails come through Siberia. I expect my term of service will expire next year, when I shall be allowed a furlough, and, if I am not blown to pieces by the Nihilists, shall probably visit the States."

"You will find us at home," said the Professor; "and I need scarcely say, you will have a hearty welcome."

They landed with him; and the last they saw of their friend was as he stood, with his Aino servant, on a rocky plateau near the waterfall, with his gun upon his shoulder, watching them, as they were rowed back to the ship.

The man-of-war steamed directly for Soya, and, after taking

HUROI, SOUTH-EAST COAST OF KARAFUTO.

in a supply of fresh water, proceeded down the eastern coast of Yezo to Yesashi, where the travellers went on shore.

Oto discovered an old friend in the Japanese officer of the Kaitakushi, who was endeavoring to make agriculturists of the Yezo-jin. His name was Kanaya; and, having been educated at Yale, he was really overjoyed to once more meet Americans.

"I am engaged upon a kind of missionary work," he laughingly remarked to the Professor. "The Yezo-jin are like children. They begin very diligently, break up the ground, and plant it just as I teach them; but in two or three days their curiosity gets the better of them, and they dig up the seeds to ascertain their progress. I think that shows how impossible it is to do any thing with them."

Fitz chuckled, and said, —

" Well, if such an act indicates lack of intelligence, I am afraid that I must be very little better than your pupils."

" And I," said Sallie.

" I believe such curiosity is an inherent weakness of human nature," said the Professor. " Even scientific men will sometimes unearth a seed in order to see how its germination is developing."

Fitz nodded assent, and said very gravely, —

" Yes, we all do it."

This made Mr. Kanaya laugh, and say, —

" Well, sir, and pray of what science are you the professor?"

" Of fun," said Johnnie. " He enjoys it more than any boy I know."

" Well, my larks never did anybody harm," remarked the merry fellow. " You know what mother says, — it is better to laugh than to cry."

The Professor was about to make one of his characteristic speeches, when his wife whispered to him, —

" Do not lecture, pa: you must save yourself for your winter course."

The gentleman took the hint, and said, —

" Mr. Kanaya, I can quite sympathize with you, for I have had to instruct young Americans who were just as inquisitive as your Yezo-jin. By the way, do you think you could commu-

nicate with old Poro Parumbe, one of the chiefs who conducted
us from Hokuyak-bets? I believe we are in his district."

"Poor old man!" said Mr. Kanaya, "I have bad news to tell
you about him. When he reached home, he shared the cask of
sugar you gave him, between Kure Kina, Taiki Kamoi-yashi,

PORO PARUMBE'S CANDY-PULL.

and Setta-eye, and gave a big feast to his tribe. He placed his
portion of the sugar in an iron pan, and boiled it into candy,
which I instructed them how to pull. The result was, he ate
too much, and died the next day."

"What a sweet ending!" said Fitz. "Guess he was not
used to taffy."

"Do not jest upon such a solemn subject," said his father,

who imagined, from the boy's twinkling eyes, that he was about to further express his opinion. "No doubt, the late chief's relatives felt grieved at his untimely decease."

"It did not seem to trouble them," said Mr. Kanaya. "As soon as the old fellow was buried, the tribe assembled, and elected another leader."

"Yes," said Fitz to Sallie. "Do you remember, when Mr. Tony Jones the selectman died, the politicians in Cromlech wore badges bearing the legend, 'We mourn his loss:' then, when the funeral was over, they went straight to the Town Hall, and elected George Skinner Flynt. I guess human nature is about the same everywhere. But, sis, you had better take warning by the fate of Chief Poro Parumbe, and not eat too many caramels."

"Do not talk about caramels, Fitz," she answered: "it makes my mouth water."

"Well, I'd kinder like to interview a box," he drawled. "After all, there is no place like the States; is there, Sallie?"

"No, indeed," she answered.

"As our old guide is no longer living, I think we might call upon his successor," said the Professor. "Does he reside far from here?"

"Hokuyak Namihu is a great hunter," answered Mr. Kanaya. "He is constantly on the move. The Ainos are beginning to set their fox-traps, and the chief will possibly be down at Takoni-bets."

They camped on shore, and, at daybreak the next morning, started in boats. Towards noon the sun became very hot: so Mr. Kanaya landed, and cut some *beckonishita* leaves which he distributed to his guests. As the Ainos resumed their poling, the official made an awning of one of the leaves; and looked so comical, crouching under it, that Oto made a sketch of him.

"That is clever," said Sallie. "You can almost hear Mr. Kanaya saying to the Aino, 'Move that iron kettle off those rice-bags: I do not want the latter cut, and the contents spilt into the bottom of your boat.'"

"Look at that bird!" cried Fitz, pointing to a curiously

USING A BECKONISHITA LEAF.

crested species of hoopoe, flying overhead. "Is it not a comical creature?"

Johnnie, who carried a fowling-piece, raised his weapon, and fired; his prize tumbling right into the bow of the boat.

"That was well done," said the Professor. "You timed your fire with mathematical precision."

"Oh! that was only a fluke, sir," said Fitz.

"A what?" was the stern query. "I believe a fluke is that portion of an anchor which secures it in the ground. It is also a term applied to the points of a whale's tail; and to the *distoma hepaticum*, a parisitic cotyloid entozoön, with a flat lanceolate body and two suckers, found in certain organs of the *ovis aries*, or common sheep."

" I did not speak of any thing as scientific as that, sir," said Fitz. " The fluke I referred to is a term used in billiards, and means an accidental lucky shot."

" I never play billiards," replied his father.

" I wish you would," said Mrs. Jewett. " It would be a good thing for you."

YEZO HOOPOE.

" Here we are at our destination," said their guide. " Now we have to disembark, and be carried about a mile by the Yezo-jin; the road-bed being up a cañon that is now full of water."

" We can walk," said Mrs. Jewett; " and I am sure the gentlemen can."

" Certainly," added her husband. " We shall, no doubt, land upon a very beautiful plateau after we get through this pass."

Their guide was amazed at the way the Americans contrived to jump from stone to stone, and he said he did not wonder that they had been able to penetrate through the heart of Yezo.   At the last turn in the cañon, they beheld a curious overhanging mass of granite, which looked as though it were about to fall upon them.

OLD TIME'S ROCK.

"That is like Profile Rock in the White Mountains," remarked Sallie. "Whose face do you think it resembles?"

None of the party guessed the same person; and at last Fitz, with his usual smartness, exclaimed, —

"Let us name it Old Time's rock."

"Good!" cried all but Mr. Kanaya, who, turning to the boy, inquired, —

"Who is Old Time? One of your prominent men?"

"Yes: he has been before the public a great many years," was the ready response; "and nobody seems to know how old he is.   Some say four or five thousand, and others billions of years."

The official gazed at the boy with astonishment, then observed, —

"I understood that he was an old man."

"Oh! he is like your Fuku-roku-jin" (one of the seven gods), — "a type or figure of speech, an ideal person, the embodiment of a long period; and is generally depicted as an aged gentleman, scantily costumed in a white scarf, carrying a scythe in one hand, and an hour-glass in the other. We do not make images of him, and worship him as you do Fuku-roku-jin."

"I do not worship that god," gravely answered the Japanese. "I thought you understood that we regard The Seven Benevolent Ones very much as you do Old Time. I now comprehend your remark. Time measures our lives with his hour-glass, and cuts them short with his scythe."

"Excuse me, Mr. Kanaya," said Fitz. "I did not wish to annoy you;" then, pointing ahead, cried, "Hullo! see that animal with its head in a bucket."

. As he spoke, one of the natives rushed forward, and despatched the creature with a club.

"That is an Aino fox-trap," said Mr. Kanaya. "The interior of the bucket is studded with sharp spikes pointing downward; and the trap is baited with seal-flesh, of which the foxes are very fond. Once the creature gets its head well in, he cannot withdraw it; and the pain makes him lose all his caution, and renders him a very easy prey."

"I call it a mean act," said Sallie. "The fox does not suspect the danger; and when he is blindfolded the Aino sneaks up, and takes advantage of the poor thing's painful position."

"Trapping any thing is an underhand way of hunting game," said Johnnie. "It is a great deal better to shoot them, and end their misery."

"Suppose you were hungry, and had no gun or other

weapon?" queried Fitz. "I do not believe, under those circumstances, even you or Sallie would go without supper."

"Yes; but they will not eat that fox," retorted his brother.

"Oh, yes, they will!" said Fitz, winking. "I tell you there

AINO FOX-TRAP.

will not be a morsel of it left to-morrow. Am I not correct, Mr. Kanaya?"

"Quite," was the answer. "The Yezo-jin, like our wrestlers, are very partial to fox-meat."

The party rested at a spring, and had luncheon, while some of the Ainos went in search of Hokuyak Namihu. Before the meal was over they returned, and delivered a long message to their employer, who appeared exceedingly annoyed with the communication.

" What is the difficulty ? " inquired the Professor.

" Oh, these Ainos are nothing better than animals ! " answered the official. " My man tells me he has found the chief; and that the latter, instead of coming to us, says he is tired, and we must go to him."

" I cannot see any thing very unreasonable in his request," answered the Professor. " As chief of his tribe, he expects a certain amount of respect; and we, being intruders, ought to call upon him."

This remark did not suit Mr. Kanaya, who exclaimed, —

" Indeed, sir, you do not understand my position. As a representative of the Kaita-kushi of the Hokkaido, I cannot permit such insolence."

" Well," was the good-natured response, " then we will go alone."

Mr. Kanaya soon recovered his usual good temper, and laughingly remarked, —

" I could not think of your doing that, Professor. The fact is, the fellow drinks too much *saké* : so I thought his message might have been the result of his excess. After all, as Confucius says, one loses dignity by being angry. Come, we will proceed to visit the chief."

They found Hokuyak Namihu in a hunting-tent, something like an Indian *tepee*, crouched behind a fire, and giving directions to one of his people, who was about to cut up a deer which was placed on an enormous *beckonishita* leaf. He was a good specimen of the Yezo-jin, and was as hairy as his namesake.

Upon noticing the strangers, he rose, bowed, and said in a very gentle voice, —

"When I was hunting this morning, the deer kicked me severely, and I am unable to walk: please excuse my not going to you as I would like to have done."

CHIEF HOKUYAK NAMIHU.

"I am sorry that I was hasty," said the young official. "It never does to place too implicit confidence in a verbal communication. We Japanese have a saying, 'Two mouths will distort the meaning of any message.'"

The chief willingly submitted to Oto's examination. "Three of his ribs are broken," said the young doctor. "It is wonderful how these Ainos bear pain. Please tell him he must remain quite quiet for several days, and not lie upon the injured side."

"You ought to have brought some of your honorable plasters," said Fitz. "I advised you to do so."

The doctor smiled, and replied, —

"To tell you the truth, I did; but I missed them when we were among the Colletské."

"Perhaps the natives took them for some kind of preserved provisions," said Fitz; "or they may have kept them as charms."

"Possibly," said Oto. "I have heard of an African negro worshipping a porous plaster."

"Aunt Cynthia Ann does that," said Fitz. "She buys them by wholesale, and gives them to the tramps."

"She might do worse," laughingly answered the doctor.

He then told the Aino how to take care of himself, and, rejoining his party, started for Yesashi.

They staid on shore two days, and would have remained longer, had not Capt. Imadate notified them that a change was about to take place in the weather, and they had better re-embark; upon learning which, they bade adieu to Mr. Kanaya, and returned to the man-of-war.

On their way down the coast they touched at Yuhito, Awashiri, Shiritoya, and Nemoro, then started for Hakodate, at which port they arrived on the 1st of November.

It was quite delightful to receive a budget of letters from home, and to be in a place where they could sit on chairs, and enjoy the society of old friends.

"Children," said the Professor, who had been perusing a communication from Tokio, "I have some news for you. The Japanese Government has kindly consented to my going home by the next steamer, which leaves Yokohama on the 15th of this month. You must have all your treasures packed and on board Capt. Imadate's ship in twenty-four hours, as he leaves for the South to-morrow evening."

"Oh! am I not glad?" said Sallie. "How I do long to see old Cromlech!"

"And I," said her parents and brothers. The news from their native place had made them all homesick, and even the Yezo roses had no charm for them.

Setta-eye had kept his word, and had sent on the skins of the bears they had killed, and many other furs, with a large number of Aino productions, such as bows and arrows, *'inaho*, etc.

As the party was about to embark, they heard a cry, and saw Habo, who was carrying something like a child on her back, and shouting in Japanese, —

"*Tomare, tomare!*" (Stop, stop!)

She did not wait until the boat backed in, but waded out to it, and, depositing her burden, saluted them in her graceful fashion, saying, —

"*Saramba, saramba!*" (Farewell!)

Fitz, for whom the present was intended, unfastened the bundle, then, as he glanced at its living contents, excitedly exclaimed, —

"'Rah! If it isn't a bear!"

CHAPTER XVII.

HOMEWARD BOUND.

"No matter how beautiful the scenery or how hospitable may be the people of a foreign land, the traveller forgets all these things, when, after a long absence, he beholds the shore of his native country."

CAPT. IMADATE kept his word, and landed them at Yokohama within the time he had promised. They bade him good-by with great regret; he having been most kind, patient, and courteous to them all.

They found their servants awaiting them on the *hatoba*, and were greeted as though they had just returned from a land inhabited by cannibals.

The Jewetts visited their friends on the bluff, then took the first train for Tokio, and that night slept in their old residence in the Kaga Yashiki.

The next week was devoted to farewell calls; and, but for the prospect before them, the young people would have felt sorry that their sojourn in the Land of the Rising Sun had drawn to a close.

Mr. and Mrs. Nambo, and Oto, spent the greater portion of the time with them; the dear old lady being much grieved at the thought of their approaching separation.

"I know she feels badly because she has not converted Sallie to Buddhism," said Fitz. "She is a sweet soul, and really believes what she preaches."

On the morning of their departure Oto's mother announced

that she had had a dream, and that she was certain her friends would arrive home in safety, and enjoy long and prosperous lives.

" I had just fallen asleep," she said, "when I saw the gods of luck assembled in consultation. All the seven were present, — Dai-koku Sama with his hammer, Bishamon Sama in full armor, Hotei Sama with his beautiful fat form, Juiro Sama with his wise face, Benten Sama lovely and radiant, Yebisu Sama looking just as he does when he is about to land a big fish, and the venerable and benevolent Fuku-roku-jin Sama, with his staff, and with the stork of longevity standing on his honorable left hand. Something was evidently pleasing the gods, for they were all laughing very merrily. Hotei Sama, being president, was the first to speak ; and he said, —

" ' Usually we do not concern ourselves with the doings of foreigners, who, I regret to say, have, with some honorable exceptions, treated us very disrespectfully.'

" ' Yes,' said Bishamon Sama : ' they have induced our faithful people to discard the ancient armor and art of warfare, to put on tight *kimono*' " (clothes), " ' and to use weapons unknown to their honorable ancestors.'

" ' They have been wise to do that,' said Fuku-roku-jin Sama. ' You must fight demons with their own weapons.'

" ' I agree with you,' said Dai-koku Sama. ' Formerly I used to tell my believers, " If you wish to have rice in your storehouse, and money in your purse, you must labor for it as a miner does with his hammer." Now I advise them to use steam, electricity, or any other invention that will keep them among the front rank of nations.'

" ' And I,' said Juiro Sama, who was leaning with his face upon his hands, ' give them the same counsel. What do you say, Yebisu Sama ? '

MRS. NAMBO'S DREAM.

"The god chuckled, then replied, —

"'I always tell them, "If you cannot catch a fish with a hook, use a spear." Is that right, Benten Sama?'

"The female god cast a languishing glance at her interrogator, then, bowing, answered, —

"'I must confess that I admire the foreigners. Although, as Hotei Sama has observed, they are not quite as respectful as he would like them to be, still they possess many virtues, among them being the esteem in which they hold my sex.'

"'We know all about that, Benten Sama,' slyly retorted the president. 'What I particularly wish to refer to is this. Some Americans, who have lived for several years in our country, learned our language, and studied our literature, and have travelled, not only through the heart of Dai Nihon, but also in Yezo, and the distant island of Karafuto, are about to return to their native land. I therefore propose that we present them with a proof of our interest in and friendship for them. What form shall it take?'

"Juiro Sama produced a *kakémono*, the silk panel of which had never been touched with ink, and, handing it to Hotei Sama, said, —

"'There is one wish that is always appropriate, and is understood by the people of all nations. Let Dai-koku Sama inscribe it upon the *kakémono!*'

"'*Hai !*'" (Yes) "cried the gods. '*Hai-hai-hai !*'

"Dai-koku Sama called for an ink-stone and a brush, and, dipping the latter in the liquid, wrote the character '*Kotobuki*'" (literally, "I hope you will enjoy long life and happiness"). "When he had made the last stroke, he held the brush towards Hotei-Sama, saying, —

"'Have you any thing to add to that?'

"The god laughed until his whole body quivered, then he replied, —

"'Nothing, Sama. Your writing is as perfect as the wish.'"

Mrs. Nambo, bowing, added, —

"After that I awoke."

"We are exceedingly obliged to you, dear friend," said Mrs. Jewett. "What more could we desire than the blessing written upon the *kakémono* you saw in your dream? If we all enjoy that, we shall indeed be fortunate. May you also have like happiness!"

The old lady sank upon her knees, placed the palms of her hands upon the mats, and, having performed the respectful salutation, murmured, —

"I am entirely unworthy of such a compliment."

"Come along, mother," shouted Fitz from the veranda. "Our *jin-riki-sha* are at the door. I have got my bear in mine. Sallie's pugs are in hers. Johnnie has a box of books, and some old *raku* bowls; and father is hidden from sight in manuscripts. Please hurry up! Our men are going to race to the Shimbashi station. Mind you hold on tight when they turn the corners."

"Old Choso will not go too fast with me," replied his parent, as she quitted the house; adding, when she turned to take a last glance at her servants, who were kneeling in the veranda, " *Saïonara, Saïonara !*" (Farewell.)

" *Saïonara !*" sadly chorused the domestics.

The run down to the railway-station was accomplished quickly; the only detentions being caused by the Professor, who, several times, insisted upon alighting from his vehicle, and performing the modern Japanese salutation to some official.

"I am sure we are late, pa," said Mrs. Jewett. "I do not

see the good of your bobbing and scraping in that way. You are not a Japanese."

"It pleases them, my dear," he replied. "Remember that I am going to lecture upon the manners and customs of these people, and I must practise their bow in order to create a sensation when I make my appearance on the platform."

Oto and a great crowd of friends were waiting to accompany them to the port; and, when the train glided from the Shimbashi platform, they were loudly cheered.

The journey occupied about forty minutes; and at Yokohama they were met by other friends, who saw the travellers down to the *hatoba*, and on board the "City of Peking," where they were welcomed by genial Capt. Friel, who said, —

"You are just in time! In another moment I should have been compelled to start without you."

Then came hand-shakings, and *saïonara* on the part of native and foreign friends, the shrill blast of the steam-whistle, and a perceptible motion of the vessel; Oto being the last to grasp their hands.

"*Saïonara*," he murmured, "*O genkini shetai oide nasai.*" ("Farewell! Continue in good health.")

The sun was setting as the ship steamed down the Bay of Yedo. When the travellers caught the last glimpse of glorious Fuji-yama, Sallie exclaimed, —

"Good-by, Fuji San. We have seen lots of mountains, but none as beautiful and majestic as you are. May you long be beheld and worshipped from the thirteen provinces!"

"Yes," added Fitz. "It would be a very sad thing if Fuji were to disappear some night, just as it appeared, all in a hurry, 'a many years ago.' I have only one regret in leaving Japan: that is, we have not ascended Fuji's sacred cone."

"I am not sorry," said Johnnie, in a musing tone. "I did quite enough Alpine-club business in Yezo."

Mrs. Jewett and the Professor stood together; abaft and the former said, —

"I am thankful that we are really homeward bound. Of what are you thinking, husband?"

"Of a title for my first lecture," he replied. "I fear that the sweet, do-nothing life we have been leading in Japan will have unfitted me for the worry and excitement at home."

They had fine weather all the way across, and reached the Golden Gate exactly seventeen days from the time of quitting Yokohama.

The Jewetts remained a few hours in San Francisco, then started across the continent; and after a week on board the cars were landed at the Cromlech depot, where they were regarded with profound interest by the loungers, whose chief occupation was to see the trains arrive and depart.

"We-ll, I wa-ant to know," drawled one long specimen, saluting the boys with a jerk of the head. "Is that a b'ar you've got there, Fitz Jewett? W'ar hev yer bin tew, all these years?"

The boy did not reply, being too intent upon seeing his prize stowed in the express-wagon.

They entered their carriage, and drove along the well-remembered road, stopping every now and then to greet old friends, who had a hundred questions to ask in a minute.

At last they ascended the crest of the hill, and beheld their home. In a brief space the Jewetts were once more under their own roof, and feeling as though they never wished to leave it again.

.   .   .   .

The boys are now at college, and Habo's gift is the terror and admiration of all who visit Cromlech. There is some talk of sending the animal to the Central-Park menagerie; but whenever the question is mooted, Fitz always interposes the plea,—

"I do not believe the poor little fellow would be happy if he could not see some of us; and remember, sir, he is the only living link between us and our old friends, 'The Bear-Worshippers of Yezo.'"

DAI-BI.

[THE END.]

www.ingramcontent.com/pod-product-compliance
Lightning Source LLC
Chambersburg PA
CBHW021216270326
41929CB00010B/1147